A TRIBUTE TO THE
PROPHET MUHAMMAD

A TRIBUTE TO THE
PROPHET MUHAMMAD

Edited by Hakan Kosova

Light

New Jersey

10 09 08 07   1 2 3 4

Published by The Light, Inc.
26 Worlds Fair Dr. Unit C
Somerset, New Jersey, 08873, USA

www.thelightpublishing.com

Library of Congress Cataloging-in-Publication Data

A tribute to the Prophet Muhammad / edited by Hakan Kosova. -- 1st ed.
    p. cm.
Includes bibliographical references and index.
ISBN 978-1-59784-077-4
1. Muhammad, Prophet, d. 632--Appreciation. 2. Muhammad, Prophet, d. 632-
- Devotional literature. I. Kosova, Hakan.
BP76.2.T75 2007
297.6'3--dc22

                                2007001096

Printed by
Çağlayan A.Ş. Izmir, Turkey
April 2007

TABLE OF CONTENTS

PREFACE

I have not praised Muhammad with my words;
rather, my words are praiseworthy because of him.

Hassan Thabit

"Tribute" is an elegant word. It connotes the quality of one's character, with graciousness and it fosters emotions of "respect" and "admiration." It is the outcome of the virtuous feeling of gratitude and one is expected to "pay" a tribute to another in return for what they have received.

In today's world "tribute" is most needed. Along with other concerns and fears, the "cartoon crisis" presented a dramatic example of how an image can be destroyed, corrupted, and publicized globally. No one is in favor of violent demonstrations or the destruction of property, but at the same time no one is in favor of the arrogant indifference to the sensitivities of Muslims and their sacred beliefs. The tension between disrespectful behavior and uncontrolled reaction defames to a greater extent the concepts and personalities that societies respect. There have been many protests from sensible leaders, academics, and clergy in the West, while many others in the East have called for tranquility. The discourse of "freedom of speech" has been manipulated to spark turmoil at a time when many people struggle to find common grounds so as to avoid a potential clash of civilizations. We are not wondering whether all this has been triggered as a part of a global conspiracy, or whether it is because we have sacrificed our sanctities for the sake of sarcasm, or free press, rather, we are concerned that such atrocities might harm and obstruct sincere efforts of dialogue and mutual respect, which are the precious hopes for a peaceful future.

It is time to rediscover the divine message that has been bestowed upon us by God Almighty . . .

It is time for the entire world to pay tribute to the Prophet Muhammad, peace and blessings be upon him . . .

It is time to devote a most deserved admiration to him. . .

It is time for both Muslims and non-Muslims alike to restore his image and message back on the most exalted pedestal where he belongs.

It is time to learn how to overcome prejudices with an open heart.

This volume in your hands is devoted to the blessed memory of the Last Messenger on the occasion of Mawlid al-Nabi. Articles contributed by scholars from around the world discuss different aspects of the Prophet and try to present us with a true image, an image that is not duly appreciated in our world today. Our hopes are that it will serve mutual understanding and intellectual enlightenment.

ACKNOWLEDGMENTS

We are thankful to the following scholars and authors for their contribution in the growth of this work: M. Fethullah Gülen (*The Fountain*), Kathleen St.Onge (*The Fountain*, Canada), Alphonse Dougan, PhD (*The Fountain*, USA), Sermed Ogretim PhD (*The Fountain*, USA), Yetkin Yildirim, PhD (University of Texas), Thomas Petriano, PhD (St. Joseph's College, NY), Kerim Balcı (journalist, *Aksiyon*, Ankara), T.J.Winter (Cambridge University, UK), Hasan Horkuc, PhD (University of Durham, UK), Mehmet Erdoğan (poet, Kaynak Publishing Group, Istanbul), Ali Fuat Bilkan, PhD (TOBB University, Ankara), Kutlukhan Shakirov, PhD (editor – *Noviye Grani*, Istanbul).

THE PROPHET MUHAMMAD

A SHORT BIOGRAPHY

Hüseyin Algül

The Prophet Muhammad was born on Monday 20 April 571, on a Monday, in the city of Mecca. He was born into the Hashim family which was a branch of the noble and powerful Quraysh tribe. His father, Abdullah, was a tradesman, and he died before the Prophet was born. His mother, Amina, lived until he was six. For two years, the blessed orphan was taken care of first by his grandfather Abdulmuttalib, and later by his uncle Abu Talib upon the grandfather's will.

The last Prophet was the fruit of Prophet Abraham's prayer, Jesus' glad tidings, and his mother Amina's dream. After building the Ka'ba, the Prophet Abraham prayed to God "Our Lord! Raise up among that community a Messenger of their own, reciting to them Your Revelations, and instructing them in the Book (You will send to him) and the Wisdom, and purifying them (of false beliefs and doctrines, and sins, and all kinds of filth.) Surely, You are the All-Honored with irresistible might, the All-Wise" (Baqara 2:129). Jesus told those around him of the Prophet who would follow him called "Ahmad." Muhammad's mother, Amina, had a dream in which she was told the following:

> "You carry in your womb the lord of this people; and when he
> is born say: 'I place him beneath the protection of the One,
> from the evil of every envier'; then name him Muhammad."

The Prophet's birth was a sign of the acceptance of this prayer, the manifestation of these glad tidings, and the realization of this dream.

The Prophet's father departed for another city for reasons of trade, whereupon he became ill and died. He was buried in Medina. Thus, the Prophet Muhammad never saw his father. From the time of his birth until he was four years old, he stayed with his wet-nurse, Halima. He then stayed for another two years with his mother Amina. When he was six, his mother took him to Medina to meet his relatives and to visit his father's grave. Because Salma, the mother of the Prophet's grandfather, Abdulmuttalib, was from Medina, they had relatives in this city. The grave of the Prophet Muhammad's father was in the garden of his uncles' house in Nabiga. Amina visited the grave of her husband, Abdullah, and the Prophet became acquainted with his relatives from the Najjar tribe. On the return journey, Amina became ill and died in Abwa, where her body was laid to rest. Umm Ayman brought the Prophet to Mecca, whereupon he came into his grandfather's care. He stayed with his grandfather from the age of six until he was eight. When the Prophet's grandfather died, according to his will, Muhammad went to stay with his paternal uncle, Abu Talib. Abu Talib was a respected person in Mecca, and he was known as the most esteemed of Abdulmuttalib's sons.

The Prophet Muhammad's loss of his parents and grandfather during his childhood did not destroy his fortitude. He herded his uncle's sheep to pasture in Mecca. He carried every task at home with great joy and contributed to the family budget. His aunt, Fatima, treated him as her own and he never upset her. In those years, wherever the Prophet was living, even the house of his wet-nurse, found itself in plenty. As a matter of fact, although Abu Talib was not a wealthy person in those years, after the Prophet came to stay, it became apparent that he was a source of blessings for the household.

When he turned 13 he joined his uncles in trade. He was involved in trade for many years, and became known for his honesty and principles. When he was only 20, he joined an institution called *Hilf al-Fudl* (the alliance of the virtuous) set up by some Meccan people to combat thieves, robbers, brigands, oppression, and injustice; he was a very effective member. When he was 25, he married Khadija. Khadija was forty at that time and her decision to marry him was influenced primarily by his reputation as "*al-Amin*" (the trustworthy, the honest). When he was 35, the tribes in Mecca began to reconstruct the Ka'ba. At the end of the project, a disagreement erupted, for each tribe wanted to have the honor of placing the Black Stone back in the Ka'ba. They asked Muhammad "the trustworthy one" to arbitrate the dispute. He put the stone on a ground cloth and had each tribe hold one corner. This prevented a serious conflict and further established his potential to be a leader.

When the Prophet approached the age of forty, he experienced a desire to distance himself from people and to go out into the country to seek seclusion and to contemplate nature. He had lived an untainted childhood and youth. Now, looking back, he was deeply saddened by the corruption and amorality in the lives of the people around him. Because of this, he began to stay for certain periods in a cave called Hira on Mount Nur, near Mecca. There he would stay for a while and then return to the city. Once, on the return journey, he heard a voice call out from among the rocks and trees: "O, Muhammad!" It was subsequent to this that he started to have dreams that would be realized the next day.

In 610, when he was 40 years old, during the month of Ramadan the Archangel Gabriel came to him and the period of his revelations began. The first revelation was the verse that begins "Read, in the name of the Creator, God…" This is how Almighty God gave the duty of Prophethood to Muhammad.

The first people to accept the Prophet's invitation to Islam were Khadija, Ali, Zayd ibn Haritha and Abu Bakr. They were followed by Uthman, Abdurrahman ibn Awf, Sa'd ibn Abi Waqqas, Talha and Zubayr. Those first Muslims, in particular the Prophet, underwent great torment at the hands of the idol worshippers. In fact, many Muslims, like Yasir and his wife, Sumayya, were murdered after unbearable tortures. Bilal al-Habashi, Abu Fukayha, Habbab ibn Arat, and Umm Abis, Nahdiyya and Zinnira also underwent great torment. These were people who were held in low esteem by the idolaters;

even the slaves and servants of these Muslims underwent many hardships.

The resistance of these first Muslims greatly affected the spread of Islam. As a matter of fact, during the first six years of his Prophethood, strong and brave men like Hamza and Umar embraced Islam and found their place among the Companions of the Prophet. As the number of those who believed in Islam increased, so did the number of obstacles placed by the idolaters to prevent the spread of this new faith. In the fifth and sixth year of the Prophethood, some Muslims were forced by the situation to attain permission from the Prophet to emigrate to Abyssinia. In the seventh year the unbelievers isolated the Muslims in one area and boycotted them. They were banned from trade, travel, and interrelations with other people. This situation lasted for three years. In the tenth year of the Prophethood, with the successive deaths of Khadija and Abu Talib, the torment and suffering caused by the enemies of Islam increased yet again. Khadija and Abu Talib were respected people in the community and this respect had, to some extent, provided a degree of protection for the Prophet. At this time, the Prophet Muhammad went to Taif to try to gain some outside support. But the people of Taif not only refused Islam, they rejected and stoned the Prophet. He was only able to save himself by taking shelter in an orchard outside Taif, where he sat covered in his own blood. In his supplication after having undergone this horrible treatment, the Prophet said that if he were truly fulfilling his mission then such torture meant nothing to him. It is without a doubt that he acted correctly and that he fulfilled his responsibilities.

At this time, those who ruled Mecca reached a decision that the Prophet should not be allowed back into the city. For this reason, he turned to Mut'im ibn Adiyy to attain protection to enter Mecca. It was a commonly observed tradition at those times among the prominent people of the Quraysh tribe that one could ensure security by attaining their protection.

While these successive torments rained down on his head, the Prophet Muhammad embarked on his heavenly journey, Mi'raj. The

Prophet ascended to the presence of the Almighty where he was blessed to receive divine commandments without mediation. It was on this night that the Prophet brought down many of the rules that are found in sura Isra, the seventeenth chapter of the Qur'an; 12 of the commandments found between the 22 and 39 verses of sura Isra were revealed on this night. These 12 commandments are listed as follows:

1. Be a servant to no one but God.
2. Treat your parents well.
3. Ensure the rights of your relatives, the poor, and travelers.
4. Be neither mean nor wasteful.
5. Do not kill your children due to a fear of poverty.
6. Do not approach adultery or fornication.
7. Do not kill.
8. Do not abuse the property of orphans (do not use it in an incorrect manner).
9. Keep your promises.
10. Take care to use correct measurements and weights.
11. Do not pursue things of which you have no knowledge.
12. Avoid pride and conceit.

The bestowal of such a wonderful miracle through the Prophet Muhammad was a sign that one day Islam would flourish.

Despite the difficulties he faced, the Prophet Muhammad's efforts to spread the message of Islam continued. He intensified most of his efforts on the crossroads where travelers from outside the city might pass. Finally, a group of six people who had come from Medina (then Yathrib) for pilgrimage testified to the truth of the message he brought and they promised to fulfill the conditions of Islam. The following year, five of this group came together with seven other people from Medina and together they gave their pledge to the Prophet at Aqaba. A second pledge took place with seventy-five people who all promised to protect the Prophet as they protected their women and children. In the time that followed, the Muslims who suffered in Mecca emigrated to Medina where they found favor from God and his Messenger. In Islamic literature this is known as the *Hijra*. The last to emigrate were the Prophet and Abu Bakr. This was a very difficult emigration. The idolators of Mecca chased them from the Thawr caves to the south of Mecca, and continued their pursuit all the way to Medina. Despite this danger, the Prophet and Abu Bakr managed to reach Medina. The Medinan people, in contrast to the Meccans, took the Prophet into their bosoms. They united around him. The people of Medina supported those who had abandoned their homes in Mecca for the glory of God. It is for this reason that Almighty God calls the people of Medina the *Ansar* (the helpers) in the Qur'an. As a matter of fact, brother and sisterhood was established between the emigrants and the *Ansar* immediately after the emigration of the Prophet. In this way, the action of helping people gained a spiritual dimension in Islam. This support helped to waylay the problems the Meccan Muslims would encounter. The emigrants found the opportunity to share their experience of Islam with the people of Medina. The emigrants established shops and markets; they managed to support themselves and benefit the economic life of their new city.

All of these events frightened the idolators in Mecca. They wanted to destroy the Muslims before they had a chance to become any stronger. This resulted in many battles between the Muslims and the idolaters. The most important ones were Badr, Uhud, the Battle of the Trench, and Muraysi. Finally, in the year 630, the Muslims of Medina conquered Mecca. They cleansed the Ka'ba from idols, and reverted the Ka'ba, which was built by the Prophet Abraham, to its original state. The Prophet did not act with resentment. Rather, he issued a general pardon. Despite his strength, he showed forgiveness and thus solidified his greatness. He focused on unification and celebration; he had no time to waste on trivial matters. Upon the purification of the Ka'ba, Bilal al-Habashi, the muezzin of the Prophet, called the first noon prayer and formally announced the superiority and unity of the one and only God.

The proud and haughty tribe of Hawazin, who could not stomach these new developments, laid plans to prevent the growth of Islam.

Soon, they were defeated in their war against the Muslims., and Islam resounded throughout the Hijaz to the whole of the Arabian Peninsula. Within one year after the Prophet's return to Medina he hosted representatives from hundreds of tribes.

In 632, during the time of the Hajj, the Prophet spoke before more than one hundred thousand Muslims. Known as the Farewell Sermon, this speech was a summary of Islamic thought and presented the most perfect principles in human rights.

The beloved Prophet, he who communicated God's message; He who illustrated patience, determination, and bravery, closed his eyes to this world on Monday June 8, 632.

The period in which the Prophet lived is known as the Age of Happiness, and the Blessed Era. It was the time of the Companions who were the first to submit to the Prophet's message and to the Will of God. This generation was made up of people who were firm in their faith, knowledgeable, well-mannered, masterful, hardworking, patient, and skilled. They became role models to guide future generations.

THE BLESSED BIRTH

M. Fethullah Gülen

T he birth of the Prophet Muhammad, the Pride of Humanity, peace and blessings be upon him, can be seen in the light of being the re-birth of all humanity. Until the day the Prophet honored this world, it was not possible to discern good from evil, day from night, or the rose from the thorn. It was as if the world was the abode of universal mourning, and the cosmos was lost in chaos. Thanks to the light he cast upon existence, darkness parted from light, night suffused into day, and the universe was transformed into a book that was now legible, word by word, phrase by phrase, section by section . . . the entire cosmos had in a sense undergone a revival and had nearly attained its true value.

His honoring the world is a universal phenomenon and the greatest event for both the Earth and the Heavens. Until the day he re-established a heavenly order, interpreted the meaning beyond the veil of existence, and put forward new commentaries on the cosmos, existence in its entirety made no sense; it was devoid of soul, and it was fragmented to the point that all things appeared alien. The inanimate things were nothing but lifeless figures in a nonsensical parade, whereas the animate were being crushed under the cogwheel of "natural selection," being caught every day in a different web of death. Trapped in dark solitude, every individual was an orphan and a victim impoverished by lamenting over a series of desertions. The spell of darkness was immediately broken by the light that emanated from him; the devils were defeated, and depravities drowned. The nature of creation returned to its original state; devastation was transformed to restoration, and slumber was shaken off in order to drill for repair. Our brief calls at and departures from this world have become parades; every birth has become a wedding and every death a first night.

Since the day his glow started to caress us, the pressure of "eternal extinction" has been lifted; glad tidings of reunion have come from amiable lands to the hearts that beat with the grief of separation. Thanks to the life he breathed into our souls we have attained a consciousness about our reality and are now in touch with nature. We have made use of the ore hidden in our essence and have felt the dimension of infinity embedded within. Without him, we would not be able to discover our inner profundity nor perceive so joyously the road and destination passing through the grave to infinity as we do now. He is the one who pours love and enthusiasm into our hearts, who gives brightness to our eyes, and who prepares us for this journey to the land of eternity.

Before we embark on this mysterious journey, we look upon him as our captain and cicerone. On this shore we wait for his guidance, and only with his help can we reach our final destination. We have responsibilities to him and we cannot stay indifferent in this regard. For centuries we stayed indifferent and we exceeded the limits of respect toward him and the message that he brought.

As a matter of fact, we have tried to put our connection with him on stage with *mawlid* ceremonies. We offer candies and rose-water to our guests, and sometimes we commemorate him with songs and hymns. Nevertheless, these celebrations have never been in due proportion to his grandiosity; they do not approach even that of his servants. Can we not observe the Blessed Birth in broader dimensions, more sincerely and more somberly, for the sake of his luminous message?

Nobody desires to self-indulgently celebrate or transform holy Islam into a joyous carnival, nor does anyone have the power to do so. Yet, why should not the Islamic world commemorate his birthday, which is also their birthday and the salvation of humanity?

Modern civilization would not exist without Islamic civilization, and Islamic civilization would not have come into being if it was not for the Prophet and his message.

If it was not for Islam, which appeared with its soft, tolerant, warm colors, open to learning and rewarding thought, if Muslim scholars had not transferred the Greco-Latin culture to Europe, then the Western world would have remained in the Middle Ages. There is no question that mathematics, physics, chemistry, astronomy, geometry, and medicine all have their foundations in the East, and were all stimulated by Islam. Western civilization had to wait six centuries after Jesus to become what it is today . . . they waited and encountered Islam, by which they have been greatly influenced and the West has designed its future under this light. Although the West did not accept the essentials of Islamic thought, these essentials have had a great impact on the construction of the modern Western mind and thought.

> Whatever the world owns is a gift from him,
> All people and every individual are indebted to him
> All humanity is indebted to that innocent;
> O Lord, resurrect us with this confession!

Mehmet Akif

For centuries, we have not venerated the Prophet in due fashion and could not celebrate a proper birthday, a week or a month dedicated solely to his blessed birth. It would still not be enough if we observed years over years, nevertheless, "a king does what he is expected, and a servant observes his servanthood." Therefore, we should put in action whatever we can in this regard, whatever is within our capacity saying, "better than nothing."

---

* An abridged version of the author's article entitled "Kutlu Doğum" first published in *Sızıntı*, October 1991.

ON THE PERFECTING OF A PROPHET

Kathleen St.Onge

One of the articles of faith of Islam is to believe in the Prophet Muhammad, peace be upon him. So when anyone casts a shadow on his character, the Muslim world feels deeply antagonized. Yet some remarks are extreme in their negativity and many non-Muslims really question the Prophet of Islam—who is he, and why do Muslims embrace him so completely? When I first came to Islam from Christianity almost two years ago, I asked myself this question, too. Muslims believed in him purely from their hearts. I admired them, but I was still captive of a secular, overly rational mindset. If I were going to accept the Prophet fully, it would have to "make sense" logically.

Muslim friends told me about his hard work, his impeccable character, and his innumerable virtues. Ironically, the more they spoke of his perfection, the more I resisted. It reminded me too much of the fervor of Christians regarding Jesus, peace be upon him. Risk comes with excessive praise—inadvertently a wonderful prophet can be raised to a status higher than a mortal man. Like many current and former Christians, I would not believe that Jesus was God, and I was scared of language which elevated any prophet too highly.

So every time I read about the Prophet, I prayed for protection from my own misconceptions and cultural prejudices. Then one day, I came upon a lovely story about the infant Prophet being nursed by a Bedouin. While he lived with the tribe, they enjoyed bountiful harvests and animals full of milk. The Bedouins soon became convinced this particular baby was very special. I had seen God looking out for the children in my life and providing for them inexplicably at particularly difficult times. So, by the grace of God, the Bedouin's story opened a door for me.

Slowly, with more reading, the walls around my heart began to disintegrate. Polygamy was acceptable among Muslims, Jews, Christians, and polytheists at the time. But the Prophet had many wives, and non-Muslims eagerly cited this as evidence of perversion. What was the rational truth? First, he was loyal to his wife Khadija for 20 years, though she was his elder by 15 years. Two years after Hatice died, the Prophet married again—the destitute widow of an old friend and the daughter of his best friend and staunchist supporter.

The latter, the lovely Aisha (may God be pleased with her) was a bright, beautiful, young woman that the Prophet had known since her birth. She was one of the first converts to Islam and she remained one of his most loyal confidantes. She was also a gifted historian. Having the option to marry only her, why wouldn't he have done so? She was surely everything he could desire, physically, emotionally, intellectually, and spiritually, and he chose her company on his deathbed. Later he married others. These women were relative strangers, they were of different ages, they looked different, and they held different positions in society. They brought with them several children, and great responsibility. His marriages formed alliances between previously disparate peoples—Egyptian Copts, Jews, warring Arab tribes, and Africans. Thus, their union with the Prophet Muhammad shattered the roots of racism and social repression. The Prophet's home became the first school of Islam, as his wives and their children became ambassadors among their own peoples, thereby increasing both the acceptance and the reach of Islam. It is simply illogical to think that a man in his 50s and 60s, a man with a perfect young wife, would seek to complicate his life by adding more people to his household, just to satisfy his sexual needs. Clearly, his complex home life was part of his calling and in no way reflected deviance on his part.

The image of the Prophet as a warrior was another point of contention which I found myself debating with my own Christian relatives. For after extensive reading, my conclusion was that he was simply a man with an opinion far different from the prevalent viewpoint, and this is never easy in any place at any time. He fought to defend himself and his community, and to protect the right of himself and others to profess their faith. He did it superbly, but excellence is hardly something to hold against someone. A simple and factual look at his choices tells it best. He could have stayed at home quietly with a few children and grandchildren; he could have lived in comfort and peace. Instead, he took to the battlefield washing his body with sand, with rocks strapped to his stomach to fade the feeling of hunger. He did not become rich, nor did he retire to a leisurely life. Instead, he remained poor, tired, harassed, and threatened. He did not become the object of worship for anyone—proof is in the fact that Muslims celebrate his birth, death, and calling simply as days of reflection and prayer. The Muslim high holidays relate strictly to the message of Islam—the submission to one God—and not to the man. If he were really a megalomaniac, as those strongly opposed to Islam argue, why didn't he "invent" verses of the Qur'an to compel Muslims to recognize him as better than all the prophets and make himself the object of all prayers? Instead, he is respectfully referred to in the Qur'an as a beautiful example of humanity, an illiterate among his own people, and a simple messenger. The message is always clear—all praise is due to God, not the Prophet.

Yet in a further assault on his character, non-Muslims then and now insist that the Prophet Muhammad, peace and blessings be upon him, was fed all his information by other people and simply "rehearsed tales of the ancients." Yet this is illogical. First of all, the Prophet spent most of his time prior to his calling with salesmen, not scholars. These caravan merchants knew "a little about a lot," having traveled extensively, but they could hardly be expected to know worldly subjects deeply. Most were illiterate themselves, having an education suited strictly to trade. Yet the Qur'an contains extensive details about past communities and religious doctrines, and about geological and human history. The depth of the knowledge conveyed is too great to be simply hearsay gleaned at a fireside chat among tradesmen. This knowledge requires full-time scholarship to acquire even today, never mind 1,300 years ago when there were few texts and scientific instruments, and even fewer translations. When do his opponents suppose he would have acquired so much knowledge anyhow? This would have required daily conversations with sages in the middle of numerous battles, an incredibly busy family life, countless daily prayers, and his own mission to deliver the message to others. Yet he was never seen with any mortal teacher, and even his enemies have never suggested that he had one.

In fact, some fervent opponents insist that Muhammad was delusional—receiving inspiration from his own insanity. But if this were true, how could he simultaneously administer a massive, complex household with many wives and children, an intricate administration composed of alliances between peoples of different religious, socio-cultural, political, and economic backgrounds, and also strategize the stability of the Islamic empire for both the present and the future? The Prophet's military and political savvy are enshrined in the historical record, in volumes upon volumes published by Muslims and non-Muslims alike. And the basic reality is that he could not have been insane and infinitely pragmatic at the same time. Besides, if his only goal was to manipulate people, why didn't he have more commonly accepted tactics? Magic, for example, is easy to learn. Yet the Prophet's record, even as quoted by non-believers, is devoid of cheap illusions.

And what of the "new knowledge" contained in the Qur'an—the scientific revelations about the rotation of the earth, speed of light, layers of the atmosphere, creation of stars, separation of the oceans, types of rocks, origin of the rain, gender of plants, composition of human tissue, formation of the embryo, origin of iron, and so on? Of all the sacred books around the world, only the Qur'an contains verifiable scientific data. What mortal source could have imparted such things to the Prophet? None. And to what end? Since these facts could not be verified until very recently, what benefit were they in convincing anyone in his time? None. If the Prophet intended to persuade people with some sort of self-contrived document, why put in a lot of material that wouldn't make sense to anyone for another 1,000 years or more?

Truthfully, if he simply hoped for personal gain, for an easier life for himself, he would have been better off to just keep quiet and forget about the Qur'an completely. I see how my own life would have been much smoother with my relatives if I hadn't converted to Islam. The Prophet Muhammad had already lost his father, mother, and guardian grandfather. Why wouldn't he want to please and protect the only family he had left, his beloved uncle, and adhere to polytheism? Why wouldn't he have wanted to simply retire comfortably in Meccan society as a prosperous husband, good father, and prominent member of the community?

The fact is that the Prophet Muhammad was a hard-working, brilliant, courageous, and spiritually profound man who gave everything he had in this life to argue the faith of Islam amid tremendous opposition. He sacrificed his wealth, his family, his health, and his personal comfort. His only purpose was to convince those who would listen to worship one God, not himself. In less time than most people spend getting a basic education, he engineered the first welfare system in the world, installed a national health policy of cleanliness, good diet, and preventative care that is still valid today; he abolished slavery, eliminated female infanticide, and gender discrimination in family life and inheritance. He overthrew racism, inclined millions upon millions of potent, passionate people towards sexual conservatism, and he convinced entire nations and generations after them to abstain from alcohol. What is more, he is personally responsible for the fact that over a billion people around the world pray daily in constant remembrance of one God. With painstaking precision,

he related a divine message, some of which—the scientific truths—
meant no sense to him or anyone at the time. The Prophet was
competent in all fields of existence and achieved more than almost
anyone—some would say anyone—who has ever lived. What is more,
his accomplishments are historical facts easily substantiated by any
person who is inclined to read. Thus we can understand why Muslims
embrace the Prophet Muhammad so completely—because his life
has been, and will always be, the light which makes the path to what
is right more visible and more achievable.

DURR-I YEKTA

MATCHLESS PEARL

Sermed Ogretim

The teacher listened to the students complaining about their parents' attitudes towards them. Most of the students complained about their fathers and the great pressure they put on them. As the number of the complaints increased, his eyes filled with tears; he did not have a father to complain about. The unbearable and incomparable explosion of pain caused by the absence of his father in his childhood memories filled the void in his mind and heart. Alas, all that pain did not change anything; he was permanently disabled by not having a father

Orphans are never categorized as disabled people although they actually are. Moreover, they suffer great consequences of this neglect. It is a disability to not have a mother or father during the period of your life until the age of six; the period when you construct your inner world, when you make up sub-conscious paradigms to understand the outer world, and when you develop manners by which to express yourself among others. In other words, this is the time when you set up the connections between your material and spiritual aspects. A person whose mother is absent during their childhood is disabled in terms of being able to fully understand and experience spirituality; and a person whose father is absent in the same period is disabled in their interactions with the material world.

It was November of 1979 when I joined the world of the disabled; it was my father who disappeared. But I was too young to comprehend the situation. It took me twenty-six years to understand my state as an orphan, and to finally start thinking about the ways that I could overcome my disability. As I have difficulty in understanding and experiencing the outer world, I am not able to express my inner world in the outer one as I wish. Also, I am not able to analyze the messages I receive from other people as I am expected. The outcome of such a disconnection with other people is a failure of social interaction.

However, this disability helps me better appreciate certain things that other people do not. For example, there are many holy people whose fathers were absent during their childhood for one reason or another. The most prominent of these people were the prophets Moses, Jesus, and Muhammad, peace be upon them. Because of the absence of their fathers during childhood, one should expect them to have difficulties in their relations with others, or fail to develop strong self-esteem, both essential qualities to become a leader. Contrary to these expectations, however, all had a very successful life in realizing the goal of their missions. Each successfully conveyed the word of God to an exemplary community of believers. For each, the apparent setback of being an orphan became an advantage that assisted each in the completion of their mission. Though their fathers were absent, they were supported by their mothers, whose existence and education deeply inculcated compassion and spirituality in them. Thus, they naturally had a great potential to develop a strong bond with God and a deep compassion towards their people.

In the life story of the Prophet Muhammad, these facts are very clear. His father, Abdullah, died before his birth. The Prophet Muhammad was left in the care of one parent, his mother, Amina. At the age of six, he lost her too. After his mother had passed away, his grandfather Abdulmuttalib undertook his guardianship. Unfortunately, his grandfather's death came two years later. Among his uncles, Abu Talib, despite his old age and relative poverty, agreed to foster Muhammad. Sad events followed him to his adult life. Nine years after he started to teach Islam, his wife Khadija and his uncle Abu Talib both died. These two deaths came at a time when the Prophet was terribly in need of support. In the later years of his life, three of his four daughters passed away. This sequence of losses kept him constantly in the psychology of being an orphan throughout his life. Today's statistics show that a person raised under such conditions has great potential to become a future criminal, or a victim of suicide.

Aside from these tragic events, when the achievements of his lifetime are examined, one cannot help but admire him. He started to teach Islam alone, but eventually conquered the hearts of thousands. He ministered in a society where the most abominable sins were committed daily and moral values were almost non-existent; yet he was able to transform that society into people of righteousness with high moral values. He established a state that eventually sourced a civilization; and he did this despite resistance from his own tribe and other super powers of the time. It is a miracle in addition to all the others that the Prophet Muhammad was able to overcome his situation as an orphan and achieve all these great things. This is a fact that points to God as the protector and educator of this orphan.[1]

It has been about 1,400 years since the line of prophethood ended. Today, in 2006, looking at my current situation, I find myself in a struggle to overcome my disability. The similarity between my life story and the life story of the Prophet Muhammad, who is one of the most esteemed prophets, gives me the light of hope; a light that carries the warmth of compassion and the serenity of wisdom of God.

---

[1] *Your Lord has not forsaken you, nor has He become displeased. And surely what comes after is better for you than that which has gone before. And soon will your Lord give you so that you shall be well pleased. Did He not find you an orphan and give you shelter?* (The Qur'an, Dhuha 93:3-6)

TIME MANAGEMENT IN THE LIFE OF THE PROPHET MUHAMMAD

(PEACE AND BLESSINGS BE UPON HIM)

Alphonse Dougan

In the preface to his book *The 100: A Ranking of the Most Influential Persons in History*, Michael Hart noted the supreme success of the Prophet Muhammad, peace and blessings be upon him, on both the religious and secular level (Hart 1978). The Muslim community, started with four individuals: himself, his wife Khadija, his close friend Abu Bakr, and his cousin Ali. This community reached over a hundred thousand Companions by the time of his death 23 years later. Only ten thousand or so of these companions are buried in the graveyard at Medina today, as most of them died in remote lands spreading the message (Gülen 2000). Contrary to the common perception in the West, the Prophet Muhammad did not spend most of his time in battle fields or even involved in political affairs. The total number of casualties in the battles in which he participated throughout his life was less than 800 (Hamidullah). The activities that occupied most of his daily life were worship, prayers, and supplications, followed by family and community affairs, including conveying God's message to his people. While always confident of God's help, the Messenger (upon whom be peace and blessings) was also a master of skillful time management. In this article we will review some of the time management practices that he employed in his life.

Four principles emerge from a time management perspective as we examine the life of the Prophet Muhammad (Canan 1994). Interestingly, these are also the principles agreed upon by most contemporary experts of time management (Taylor 1998, Jasper 1999, Covey, Morgenstern 2000). These are:

1. Appreciation of the value of time and, consequently, making the best use of every piece of available time.
2. The guidance of a mission, a set of values, and priorities in planning every activity.
3. Establishment of a time policy or a time budget.
4. The scheduling and completion of activities within allocated time slots.

Now we will give examples of how these principles were put to practice in the prophetic tradition.

APPRECIATION OF THE VALUE OF TIME

The value of time is emphasized in many verses of the Qur'an and in many prophetic sayings. In particular, God swears by time at the beginning of the chapter Asr in the Qur'an, meaning "time through the ages" or "afternoon." It is the general opinion of the interpreters of the Qur'an that such references are intended to draw attention to those concepts and emphasize their importance. The remaining two verses of this short chapter reinforce this view: "1. By the (token of) time (through the ages)! 2. Verily man is in a state of loss. 3. Except those who believe and do righteous deeds, and exhort one another to truth and exhort one another to steadfastness." Another such oath is to be found at the beginning of Chapter 93, Dhuha or "The Morning Hours": "(1) By the morning hours, (2) And by the night when it is still." (*) The particular translation we have adopted here is by Uzunoglu (Uzunoglu 2003). Other contemporary translations of the Qur'an include Abdel Haleem (AbdelHaleem 2004) and Cleary (Cleary 2004).

In the prayer books attributed to the Prophet Muhammad we see that there are prayers for every occasion (Gülen 2000). Examples include prayers for beginning an activity, beginning a meal, ending a meal, leaving for a journey, returning from a journey, during the journey, looking in a mirror, during ill health, for rain, against excessive rain, against cold or extreme heat, when entering the bathroom, when exiting the bathroom, and countless others. From these prayers we learn that there is almost no time slot in the Prophet's life that was not occupied with a useful activity or a prayer. On one occasion the Prophet refused to greet a person who sat idly. Later, on his way back, he saw the very same person, however, this time he was occupied with an activity. He greeted him warmly. The Prophet Muhammad summarized this as follows: "The majority of humanity is at a loss as they do not recognize the value of two of God's gifts: Health and (discretionary) time" (Bukhari, *Riqaq*, 1997).

GUIDANCE OF A MISSION

After receiving the divine call, the Prophet Muhammad focused on living and conveying the message. His ultimate goal was to fulfill his mission as a servant and messenger of God. This involved two aspects: On the personal front, he spritually struggled to ascend towards the state of being a perfect human (*insan-i kamil*), a righteous servant of God. On the social front he struggled to share the faith and practices that pleased God. The Qur'an and personal communication with God shaped his values and his priorities. In his farewell sermon during his pilgrimage, he is reported to have asked tens of thousands in attendance: "Do you bear witness that I have fulfilled my mission as God's messenger?" Of course the answer was a resounding yes, accompanied by tears (Gülen 2000).

WEEKLY TIME POLICY

In a weak prophetic tradition narrated by Ibn Abbas (Canan 1998, Harf 2000), the cousin of the Prophet, the regular activities of his days are listed: "Sunday is the day for planting seeds and construction. Monday is for travel. Tuesday is for giving blood. Wednesday is for acquisition and alms giving. Thursday is for bringing community matters to the governor. Friday is for weddings and spending time with your family. Saturday is for hunting for livelihood." The authenticity of this narration is weak and therefore we cannot conclude that it is obligatory to perform these duties on these days. However, it does give the idea of designating specific days of the week for specific projects or activities. In another, stronger prophetic tradition, the Prophet was heard to say, "Seek knowledge on every Monday" (Fayz al-Qadr 1/543). Other prophetic sayings emphasize the importance of Friday as a day of festivity and the early part of Friday as the time to clean the body and care for one's clothing. Another established prophetic tradition is to fast voluntarily on Mondays and Thursdays. From the observations of his companions it has been firmly established that the Prophet, peace be upon him, established a weekly schedule with preferred activities on each day.

DAILY TIME POLICY

The most detailed information about the time management of the Prophet Muhammad is available concerning his daily schedule. Two types of activities occupied his time: The spontaneous (un-programmed) activities and the regular (programmed) activities. The spontaneous activities included giving an audience to an envoy or a representative group, meeting an urgent need, or helping a stranger who sought aid. Such activities were accommodated within the time slots not dedicated to programmed activities. Furthermore, if a representative body were to arrive in Medina for a one-off meeting, then it would be scheduled at the first available time. However, if the group was to stay in Medina for a while, then their meetings were included in the regular plan of activities. An example of such accommodation can be seen in the case of the representative group from the tribe of Thaqif. As the group was to stay in Medina for a while, the Prophet visited them and talked with them after each night prayer. When one evening he delayed his visit, the group asked him: "O Messenger of God, you did not come at the time you used to come today; you were late, what is the reason for this? (Usd al-Gaba 1/168).

REGULAR/SCHEDULED ACTIVITIES

Regular prayer times form the framework around which all other activities are scheduled. Two aspects of the Prophet's daily schedule were as follows: (1) Activities were scheduled at the same time everyday, and (2) each activity had a designated time limit.

Regular daily prayers are ordered by God at specific times (Nisa 4:103) and the Archangel Gabriel taught the Prophet Muhammad the beginning and end of the prayer times. In authentic prophetic traditions we learn that Archangel Gabriel asked the Prophet Muhammad to join him in performing each prayer at the beginning of the time period time throughout the day. The next day, they performed each prayer at the very end of its corresponding period. The Prophet said "The best of deeds in God's sight is the prayer that is performed in time" (Bukhari, *Mawaqit al-Salat*; Muslim, *Iman*). While the beginning time for each prayer period is preferred, the prayer can be done anytime between these limits. If the time limit is exceeded even by a minute, the prayer is invalidated and the person has to perform a makeup prayer in the next period. It is easy to see that regular observation of these prayer times gives a person a high level of time consciousness. It also reveals the fallacy of the view that precise timing and punctuality are modern traditions.

Various accounts of the Prophet's daily life tell us that he was very careful in the observation of his daily schedule. We understand this particularly from the observation that when the Prophet changed his schedule, this was a cause for worry in the community. For instance, one companion relates: "The Messenger of God (upon whom be peace and blessings) left his home at a time when normally nobody saw him outside." (Usd al-Gaba 1/168, cited in Canan 1994). Another one is: "The Messenger of God (upon whom be peace and blessings) ascended to the pulpit. He was never seen on the pulpit except on Fridays before." (Ibnul Maja, *Fitan*, 33, cited in Canan 1994).

NIGHT ACTIVITIES

The narrations from his companions tell us that the Prophet used to divide his night into three segments. One segment was dedicated to worship, one to his family and one segment to his personal matters. At times, he is seen as giving his personal time to his community in meeting with them and trying to address their needs.

The Prophet was observed to halt his daily activities after sunset (Mustadrak 3/461, cited in Canan 1994). This does not mean, however, that he rested for the remainder of the evening; he sometimes held meetings after evening or night prayer. As a general principle, he did not like sleeping before the night prayer or talking after it (Bukhari, *Mawaqit*, 13/23, cited in Canan 1994). His wife Aisha reports that the Prophet used to sleep during the early part of the night and wake up for worship during the later part (Ibn Maja, *Iqama*, 182, cited in Canan 1994). On exceptional circumstances, the Prophet was observed to stay awake and deal with community affairs until late hours of the night.

The night stances (*qiyam al-layl*), the hours he spent in worship, reflection, and prayers occupy an important place in the Prophet's life. He is reported to have spent on average between 2/3 to 3/4 of each night in worship, remembrance, reflection, and supplication. This corresponds to a period of 4 to 7 hours each night, depending on the season. He explains this emphasis on night prayers in the following way: "God descends to the first heaven of the earth every night and announces, 'Is there anyone who repents; I will forgive, is there anyone who prays; I will accept,' and this continues until early dawn" (Usd al-Gaba: 6/91; Ibn Maja, *Iqama*, 182, cited in Canan 1994). He also likened his night stances to those of the Prophet David: "The best nightly prayer in God's sight is that of David. He used to sleep during the early part of the night, then wake up and spend a third of the night in prayers and sleep a little again before dawn" (Bukhari, *Tahajjud*, 7; Muslim, *Siyam*, 189; Nasai, *Qiyam al-layl*, 14, available in Harf 2000).

Daytime Activities

The Prophet prohibited his companions from sleeping after the morning prayer. He used to stay at the mosque until sunrise and have group conversations with his companions. The subjects of these conversations were both religious as well as entertaining. Sometimes, they would read poetry or discuss the previous night's dreams. It is understood that these hours were spent in a felicitous way, with companions laughing at times and the Prophet smiling (Nasai, *Sahv*, 98, Muslim, *Ruya*, 23, cited in Canan 1994). The Prophet underlines the significance of these hours held for him with the following saying: "Sitting together with a group of companions and remembering God with them after the morning prayer until the sunrise is more valuable to me than fighting in the cause of God. The same is true for the hours after the afternoon prayer before sunset" (Usd al-Gaba: 2/466, cited in Canan 1994).

Following the conversation with his companions, the Prophet would then spend time with his family. On days when he was not fasting, he would have breakfast during this period. He is known to have eaten two meals each day, a late breakfast and a dinner. Towards noon, he would take a nap and encourage others to do the same, as this would help them to stay awake at night for prayers (Mednick 2002). After the noon prayers came the time for community matters. The afternoon prayer was followed by time for the family once again. In the Meccan period, the Prophet was married to Khadija for 25 years, his only wife during this time. His multiple marriages occurred after she had passed away, when he was already over 50. The reasons and occasions for these marriages form the subject of a separate article. But suffice it to say that in general these marriages could be categorized into three types: (1) Marrying the widow of a martyr to take care of her and to honor the family. (2) Marrying the daughter or other relative of a community leader to establish family ties with that community to avoid armed conflicts. (3) Marriage with a woman of a special status so that woman could become a teacher and role model for Muslim women. This third function was especially important, as the aspects of faith that pertain to special circumstances of women could only be taught by the experience of the Prophet's wives. The Prophet was observed to visit and spend equal, fixed times with his wives during his family time. Figure 1 depicts the time allowances in a regular day of the Prophet as estimated by this author.

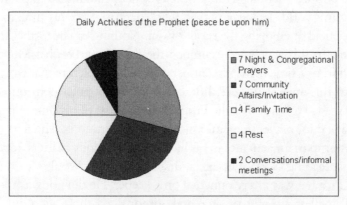

Figure 1: Estimated time allowances for various activities in a typical day of the Prophet Muhammad.

HUMAN BIORHYTHM AND ACTIVITY CHANGES

Researchers on human biorhythms tell us that multiple periodic biorhythms operate within the human body with different cycle times, changing from 90 minutes (ultradian) to daily (circadian), to longer than a day (Smolensky 2001). As the human body operates with chemicals, hormones, and electrical signals, it needs to replenish these resources once in a while (Chafetz 1992). One mechanism for achieving this is having a short break such as a nap (Rossi 1991, Mednick 2002) and another is to change one's activity when feeling tired. the Prophet Muhammad points to this important fact by saying "Relieve us O Bilal!" Bilal was the chief caller to prayer. The Prophet indicated that they were tired and less productive in the activity in which they were involved and that it was a good time to take a break and pray. "Relieve us" means "Please make the call to prayer" so the community will gather in the mosque for a congregational prayer. The interweaving of different activities in his daily schedule is another indication that the Prophet was cognizant of the effect of the biorhythm on one's productivity.

CONCLUSION

The popular mental picture of the Prophet Muhammad in the non-Muslim world depicts a person who spent most of his time in the battlefield or enjoying the spoils of war. Nothing can be further from truth. In this article we examined the life of the Prophet Muhammad from a time management perspective. The picture that emerges from this analysis is very different from the popular perception in the west. We learn that the Prophet spent most of his time engaged in worship, prayer, remembrance, and supplications. The next two most important activities in his life were community matters, including spreading God's message and family matters. We also learn that the Prophet was a very punctual time keeper. He did not waste even the smallest amount of time and admonished those who did. We learn that he kept a tight daily schedule to the extent that his companions became worried when this schedule was not observed. He designated certain days and hours of each day for certain activities. He encouraged staying awake after dawn and having a short nap at noon. He practiced such principles as eating moderately, sleeping moderately, and talking moderately, all of which ultimately help with better time management. He took advantage of every discretionary moment in life for remembering God and offering prayers. Every activity in his life was guided by his main goal of living and sharing God's religion for a happy life on the Earth and in the Hereafter. Interestingly, many of these practices are now recognized and recommended by modern experts of time management. In summary, we witness a life lived fully and productively, and yet a life that was also full of warmth and joy.

REFERENCES

- (AbdelHaleem 2004) Abdel Haleem, M.A.S., *The Qur'an: A new Translation*, Oxford University Press, 2004.
- (Bukhari 1997) M.M. Khan, *Sahih al-Bukhari: The Translation of the Meanings*, Darussalam Publishers, 1997.
- (Canan 1994) Ibrahim Canan, *Islam'da Zaman Tanzimi* (Time Management in Islam), Cihan Publiations, Istanbul:1994.
- (Canan 1988) Ibrahim Canan, *Kutub-i Sitte, Muhtasari Tercume ve Serhi* (The Six Books of Hadith, Translation and Commentary), Akcag Yayinlari, Ankara: 1988.
- (Chafetz 1992) Chafetz, Michael D., *Smart for Life*, Penguin Books, NY: 1992.
- (Cleary 2004) Cleary, T., *The Qur'an: A New Translation*, Starlatch LLC, 2004.
- (Cleary 2001) Cleary, T., *The Wisdom of the Prophet: The Sayings of Muhammad*, Shambala Publications, Boston, MA: 2001.
- (Covey) Stephen R. Covery, *First Things First*.
- (Gülen 2000) F. Gülen, "Prophet Muhammad: Aspects of His Life", Fountain Publications, VA, 2000.
- (Hamidullah 1992) M. Hamidullah, *Introduction to Islam*, Kitab Bhavan, New Delhi, 1992.
- (Hamidullah) M. Hamidullah, *The Prophet of Islam*, S. Muhammad Ashraf Publishers, Lahore, Pakistan.
- (Hart 1978) Michael H. Hart, *The 100: A Ranking of the Most Influential Persons in History*, Hart Publishing Company, Inc., New York: 1978.
- (Harf 2000) Harf Information Technology, *Hadith Encyclopedia*, contains 9 books of Hadith in Arabic, namely: Sahih Al-Bukhari, Sahih Muslim, Sunan Al-Tirmidhi, Sunan Al-Nasa'i, Sunan Abu Dawud, Sunan Ibn Majah, Musnad Ahmad bin Hanbal, Muwatta' Al-Imam Malik and Sunan Al-Darimi, Cairo, Egypt, 2000.
- (Jasper 1999) Jan Jasper, *Take Back Your Time*, St. Martin's Press, NY: 1999.

- (Mednick 2002) Sara Mednick, Ken Nakayama, Jose L. Cantero, Mercedes Atienza, Alicia A. Levin, Neha Pathak & Robert Stickgold. " The restorative effect of naps on perceptual deterioration." *Nature Neuroscience*, published online May 28, 2002.

- (Morgenstern 2000) Julie Morgenstern, *Time Management from the Inside Out*. Henry Holt & Co., September 2000.

- (Rossi 1991) Ernest Rossi, *The Twenty Minute Break, The Ultradian Healing Response*, Zeig, Tucker & Co., 1991. http://home.earthlink.net/~rossi/ultradia.htm.

- (Smolensky 2001) Smolensky, Michael, and Lamberg, Lynne, "Body Clock Guide to Better Health," Henry Holt and Co., NY: 2001.

- (Taylor 1998) Taylor, Harold L., *Making Time Work for You*, Harold Taylor Time Consultants Inc, North York, Ontario, Canada: 1998.

- (Uzunoglu 2003) Nurettin Uzunoglu, *The Holy Qur'an: Translation and Commentaries*, Islamic Publications for the Holy Qur'an Association, Istanbul: 2003.

THE ASCENSION OF THE BLESSED PROPHET

Abdal Hakim Murad

In one of the most dramatic of all hadiths, the Holy Prophet speaks as follows:

> The Buraq was brought to me. This was an animal larger than a donkey but smaller than a mule, which would place its hoof at the very horizon. I mounted it, and came to Jerusalem. I then tethered it to the ring used by the prophets. I entered the Mosque, where I prayed two rak'as. I then came out, whereupon Gabriel brought me a vessel of wine and a vessel of milk. I chose the milk, and Gabriel said: "You have chosen the *Fitra*, the natural way."
>
> He then ascended with me into the lower heavens, and requested that they be opened. A voice asked: "Who are you?" and he replied, "It is I, Gabriel." The voice then asked: "Who is with you?" and he responded, "Muhammad." And then it was said: "Is it his time for Revelation?" and he replied that it was. It was opened for us, and behold, I was with Adam, who welcomed me, and prayed for my wellbeing.

The hadith continues, describing the Blessed Prophet and Gabriel rising still further. In the second heaven they encounter Jesus and John the Baptist. In the third heaven they meet Joseph, paragon of beauty. The Prophet Enoch (Idris) greets them in the fourth. In the fifth, there is Aaron; in the sixth, Moses; and in the seventh, Abraham. Each one greets the Blessed Muhammad as a brother, and prays for him.

And then we reach the climax of the whole journey:

Then I was brought to the Lote-tree of the Boundary (*sidrat al-muntaha*), whose leaves were like the ears of an elephant and whose fruit at first seemed small. But when God spread His command over them they were so transformed that no-one in creation could describe their beauty. Then God "revealed what He revealed to me"; and He imposed upon me fifty prayers in every day and night.

The above account, related in the hadith collection of Imam Muslim, is part of Muslim scripture, and carries the authority of revelation. It is a narrative of great beauty, recalling, in some ways, Dante's *Divine Comedy*; indeed, some scholars have suggested that Dante may have been drawing on sources that were ultimately Muslim. However that may be, it is clear that the Ascension is the culminating moment of the Prophetic career. And insofar as Muhammad is "Seal of the Messengers" (*Khatam al-nabiyyin*), and the Last Prophet (*al-ʿAqib*), Muslims believe that it is the culminating moment of sacred history.

If God's Messenger is, pre-eminently, the *sahib al-miʾraj*, the man of the Ascension, then we must contemplate these hadiths as icons of the most exalted beauty and truth. The Ascension is religion at its highest, which means that every corner of these carefully painted portraits carries a deep clue about the essence of Islam.

It is striking, for instance, that the Ascension of the Blessed Prophet took place in a way which unites Mecca and Jerusalem. Mecca is the city of Ishmael, and Jerusalem of Isaac. Yet the Ismaelite Prophet, at the highest moment of his career, bridges the two. His mission, it is clear, is to close the gap between the two great branches of Abraham's family. The new religion launched in Mecca was to venerate, not scorn, the places and symbols of other prophets and other times.

People, and not only places, are to be included in this embrace. Islam does not ignore the differences between religions; indeed, the Qur'an is a statement of uncompromising prophetic truth. Yet the ascension narrative repeats again and again the Blessed Prophet's encounter with the great figures of Jerusalem's sacred history.

Christians, Muslims, and Jews may historically disagree; but the vision of the Final Prophet insists that these disagreements would be foreign to the founders of the great monotheisms. Muhammad, Jesus, Moses, and the others were uncompromising men of truth. Their affirmation of the Blessed Prophet, and therefore of each other, is not a diplomatic handshake which veils hidden ambitions and insecurities. It is utterly sincere: the final answer to those who claim that religion produces conflict and enmity. If the followers of Jesus, Moses, and Muhammad are at odds, that is not because of the teaching of their founders. It is *despite* those teachings.

Mawlana Rumi (d.1273) begins one of his greatest poems by insisting on this. But then he moves on, to a still greater theme:

> On the steed of love, God's prophet rose, through the blazing heavens,
> The messengers of God rose to salute him, noble-browed, he blessed them all.
> Gabriel himself, holding the reins, flew with Muhammad,
> Like two stars, outshining all other stars, through the dark of the trackless void.
> Then that emissary sublime called to Muhammad:
> Go alone, thy eye alone may witness where my sight would flinch and fail.
> Since his eye gazed unfaltering, he was called "the witness,"
>
> Collyrium, from 'Have We not dilated', made his vision clear and true.
> All the stations of Allah's servants by that eye were witnessed,
> Gone was the veil of self and dissipation, he saw which souls were high and base.
> Hence his intercession is sought, for he is Muhammad,
> A falcon knows all the land that lies beneath him; thus the Prophet discerns souls.

The theme of love continues. The Prophet is, as the Turkish poet Nabi (d.1712) says, "the manifestation of the light of beauty; the mirror of love and affection" (*âyine-yi hubb ü vedat*). Since all beauty is God's, and he is a perfect sign of God's qualities in this tran-

sient world, he is to be loved; and he also loves. He blesses the
prophets of old; and then, in a scene whose beauty could not be
transcended, he comes to the Station of Two Bows' Length, referred
to in the Star Sura of the Qur'an. Even the Archangel cannot reach
this rank: the beauty and closeness to the Source of Love and Beauty,
the God who is al-Rahman, the All-Merciful before He is all else,
seem to have overwhelmed him. The Prophets, in Muslim doctrine,
are better than the Angels; and Muhammad is the Refuge of all
Prophecy (*risalet-penâh*). The final degree is finally, his alone.

At that unimaginable point, the Qur'an says, *His eye faltered
not; neither did it swerve*. What did he see? The Qur'an will not say;
for the essence of Reality lies beyond the reach of language. *He saw,
of the signs of his Lord, the very greatest*. But because of his perfection,
as Best of Creation, a moment which would utterly disorient any other being does not cause his eye to "swerve." Imam al-Qushayri teaches that this signals *hifz adab al-hadra*, "maintaining the courtesies
of the divine Presence." At the supreme moment of history, the Blessed
Prophet does not flinch or fail. The luminous reality of his coming
to God is beyond our imagining; but the Book assures us that his
conduct was flawless.

This ascent 'beyond the stars' of which Rumi speaks is a mirror image of the descent like individual "stars" (*tanjiman*), which
Islamic language attributes to the miracle of Qur'anic revelation.
Only he who could rise up to that supernal point is a fitting recip-
ient for the Book which is from a world before creation, and outside the cycle of origination and death. So Fuzuli (d.1556) sings:

> You whose rising-up was the proof of your exalted rank,
> The Qur'an itself came down to earth from heaven to greet you!

The Sura of the Star, which speaks, according to most com-
mentators, both of the first "sending-down" of the Qur'an upon
the enraptured heart of the Prophet in the cave of Hira, and also of
the Prophet's ascension towards the place from which the Book was
sent, seems to allude to this. Heaven and earth are different in kind,
and the building of a bridge seems impossible. How can the Infinite

be known by the finite? How can an ant comprehend the purpose of the weaver of the carpet over which it crawls?

The Ascension gives us the astonishing news that the gulf can be bridged. There is an upward motion of the human soul, as it sheds attachments and receives the Truth more clearly in its view. This movement forms part of the harmonious yearning of all creatures for their Creator, the nightingale for the rose-garden, the river for the sea. Paralleling it is the downward movement from Unity to multiplicity. The Prophetic perfection is master of both these movements; we might say that the Prophet *is* their perfection, given that no other created entity can reach his height.

Rumi's poem reminds us of the astonishing consequences of the *nuzul*, the downward movement. Perhaps the greatest lesson of the Ascension is that the Prophet does not remain at the Station of Two Bows' Lengths. He returns to creation; not because he prefers creature to Creator—after such a voyage, how could he?—but because the beauty and mercy which he has found in God impel his compassionate nature to spread this beauty and mercy among mankind. He returns to the world, but does not seek it; he is not worldly. "Poverty is his pride." Instead, while remaining entirely human, he shines among his people as an example of the glory to which all human beings are called. Hence he is, as the Qur'an says, "a mercy to the worlds," a "shining light."

The poet Ahmet Pasa (d.1497) writes:

> Such a beloved art thou, that those that see your beauty
> find their base earth transmuted into gold, by the grace of that regard.
> Such a lamp art thou, that on the night of the Ascension,
> your discourse brought light to every one of God's creatures.

He returns not with wealth, but with light. Hence the many hadiths which speak of the mere presence of the Prophet transforming human hearts. People would sit in his company, quietly looking at him, discovering the deep transformative miracle of the beauty of the face in which there is no trace of "self and dissipation." Such a person, who has chosen the milk of nature over the wine of distraction, is a "witness," and is a proof (*shahid*) of God. According to a great prophetic poem by Nazim of Belgrade (d.1727), "Walking round the Ka'ba of your beauty is for me the surest duty." For the greatest proof, in our finite world, that there is an Infinite is the one who has made the journey into the Unknown, to bring back the joyful news that the source of creation is pure light, love, and goodness. It is that same loving witness that will intercede for sinners on the day when time comes to an end.

The hadith with which we began has a conclusion. The divine gift that the Prophet receives during the Ascension is the *namaz*, the regular Muslim prayer. The hadith explains how God commanded the Prophet that this was to be done fifty times a day by every Muslim man and woman. On his way back to the world, he meets Moses, who tells him that people will not be able to carry such a load. He humbly returns several times to the presence of God, until the number is reduced to five.

The Muslim prayer is the "ascension of the believer" (*mi'raj al-mu'min*). It contains fragrant memories of the place where it was given. To this day, when Muslims pray, they repeat the greetings which the Angels offered to the Chosen One on his ascent: "Peace be upon you, O Prophet, and the mercy and the grace of God!" Each Muslim, in this way, is reminded of that most glorious moment of the founder's life; and is invited to follow him, on the way back to the One who is the source of all reconciliation, beauty, and love.

MUHAMMAD AND JESUS
TWO GREAT PROPHETS OF GOD

Thomas Petriano

The relationship between Christianity and Islam throughout history has been often characterized by misunderstanding, rivalry, and frequently hostility. As illustrated in the recent movie, *The Kingdom of Heaven,* these tensions reached their pinnacle of ugliness during the Crusades. In today's post 9-11 world, these same misunderstandings, rivalries, and hostilities are in danger of being ignited again as extremists on both sides attempt to persuade us that Christianity and Islam are fundamentally opposed to one another. Such claims can only be overcome by persistent efforts to engage in dialogue so as to promote understanding and reconciliation. Only such sincere and honest exchange can bring about the understanding that will enable Christians and Muslims, together with Jews, to coexist peacefully in the 21st century.

This article will focus specifically on Muslim-Christian dialogue by pointing out that in the inspired vision of our great and holy founders, Jesus and Muhammad, there is far more that we share in common than there is that divides us. If Jesus and Muhammad had lived at the same time and had actually known each other, it seems from what we know of them that they would have recognized each other not as rivals, but as friends. There are four themes that I find in the gospels and the holy Qur'an that convince me that their teachings were inspired by the same fundamental faith and vision for humanity.

First of all, in each of their respective traditions, Jesus and Muhammad are beloved by God. In Islamic tradition there are several titles of honor by which the Prophet Muhammad is known. For example, he is known as *Abdullah* – "the servant of God;" *Mustafa*, "the chosen one;" and *Ahmad*, "the one who is praised." Most often, he is known as *rasool* or "the messenger." Above all, however, Muhammad is known as *habib*, "the beloved of God."

Likewise, Jesus in the New Testament is also referred to as the beloved of God:

> And when Jesus was baptized, he went up immediately from the water, and behold, the heavens were opened and he saw the Spirit of God descending like a dove, and alighting on him; and lo, a voice from heaven, saying, "This is my beloved son, with whom I am well pleased." (Matthew 3:16-17)

This same scene is repeated in the gospels of Luke and Mark, and it serves to reinforce the conviction that Jesus is indeed the beloved of God. So, for both Christians and Muslims, their founders are recognized as God's beloved. It follows then that for those who love God, whether they be Muslims or Christians, it is important to love Jesus and to love Muhammad. For God, there is no rivalry between them. They are both the beloved of God. Those who would claim to be their followers must then have the same respect and love for both of them.

Historically, Muslims have shown much greater respect for Jesus than Christians have shown for Muhammad. Muslims are very knowledgeable about the life of Jesus, and he is spoken of with great respect throughout the Qur'an. The same has not been the case for the traditional attitude of Christians toward Muhammad. Sadly, some of those prejudices continue in some circles today. This is largely because of insufficient or inaccurate information about Muhammad and his life. A better knowledge of the life of Prophet Muhammad will help Christians understand why he is also known as "the beloved of God—*al habib*."

Another similarity between Jesus and Muhammad is evident in their strong and uncompromising vision of social justice. They both recognized the inequalities and injustices that existed in their respective societies, and both of them were passionate defenders of the poor, widows, and orphans. For example, in the Qur'an, God speaks through his messenger, Muhammad, as follows:

> Alms are for the poor and the needy, and those employed to administer the (funds); for those whose hearts have been (recently) reconciled (to Truth); for those in bondage in debt; in the cause of Allah; and for the wayfarer: (thus is it) ordained by Allah, and Allah is full of knowledge and wisdom. (Tawba 9:60)

It is on the basis of passages such as this one that the concept of *zakat* became one of the five pillars of Islam and thereby an obligatory act of devotion for all Muslims. The sense of equality of all people that is derived from this principle is one of the central tenets of Islam. It is also exemplified in the various *sunnah* and *hadith* of Prophet Muhammad; for example, the honor he gave to Bilal in inviting him to be the first to chant the words of the *adhan* calling Muslims to prayer. This gesture was nothing less than revolutionary for that time and place.

Another example from the *sunnah*, as recounted by Karen Armstrong in her book *Muhammad*, is the story of a poor man who had committed a minor crime and is told to give alms to the poor as a penance for what he did. Just as the man was telling the Prophet that he did not have anything to give away, a basket of dates was brought into the mosque by someone as a gift for Muhammad. The Prophet, in turn, gave the basket to the poor man and suggested that he use those dates to distribute to the poor. The man replied that he didn't know anyone who was poorer than he was. Muhammad laughed at his response and suggested that he give the dates to his family as his penance.

Like Muhammad, Jesus frequently spoke on behalf of the poor and disadvantaged. The famous teaching of the beatitudes, which were part of the Sermon on the Mount are one example. Another is found in the Gospel of Luke, where Jesus uses the words of Prophet Isaiah to refer to himself as he reads from the scroll:

"The Spirit of the Lord is upon me because he has anointed me to preach good news to the poor. He has sent me to proclaim release to the captives and recovering of sight to the blind, to set at liberty those who are oppressed, and to proclaim the acceptable year of the Lord" And he closed the book, ...and began to say to them, "Today this scripture has been fulfilled in your hearing." (Luke 4:18-21)

Not only did Jesus preach this powerful message of love and justice for all the most marginalized members of society, but in his own actions he brought these words to life. The four gospels frequently make reference to Jesus' special compassion for the sick, the poor, and the forgotten and neglected members of his society. In Matthew, 25: 31-46, he further suggests that his disciples will be known and judged by their actions of feeding the hungry, clothing the naked, and visiting the sick and imprisoned. In fact, whenever one performs one of these actions to the "least" of his brethren, it is as if he were performing it for Christ himself. It is perhaps for this very reason that the Qur'an honors and respects Jesus. His sense of charity and justice, which is very much rooted in the justice proclaimed by the Hebrew prophets, is totally in sync with the vision of justice taught and practiced by Prophet Muhammad.

A third trait shared by both Jesus and Muhammad is their love for God. Jesus referred to God as *abba*, an Aramaic word which means "father" (or most closely translated, "daddy"), and Muhammad addressed God as Allah, the Arabic word for God. For both of them, God was the center of their lives. They lived their lives always deeply conscious of God's power and presence and of themselves as the beloved of God. The gospels speak frequently of Jesus going off by himself to pray—either into the desert, or to a mountain, or to a garden (such as the Garden of Olives where he prayed the night before he died). The spiritual writer Anthony Padavano reminds us:

He prays at every turn, on any occasion, each day, during the night, while on the water, lost in the mountains, alone in the temple, forsaken in the garden, at supper with his friends, throughout the ordeal of the cross. (from his book, *Dawn without Darkness*)

The strength of Jesus' ministry was the relationship that he cultivated with God in prayer. Jesus was a man of God because he was a man of prayer.

Likewise, Prophet Muhammad was recognized by all of his followers as a prayerful, deeply God-conscious person. The Prophet Muhammad received the first verses of the Qur'an while he was praying on Mt. Hira, and the two great moments of epiphany that Muhammad was privileged to receive, the Night of Ascent (*laylat al- miraj*) and the Night of Power (*laylat al- qadr*), are examples of his deep devotion to prayer and the deep intensity of his prayer. Indeed, of the night of power the Qur'an says: "The Night of Power is better than a thousand months." The practice of *salat* five times daily is meant to keep each Muslim aware of God throughout the hours of the day, following the example of Prophet Muhammad in his deep devotion to God and all-encompassing God-consciousness. In addition to the five times of daily prayer, there is the prayer known as *du'a*, which corresponds more to the Christian understanding of prayers of petition. From the *sunnah* and *hadith* there are many traditions relating Muhammad's devotion to prayer on many different occasions of the day and the long periods of time he often spent in *salat*. As with Jesus, the rhythm of Muhammad's daily life was one of prayer and devotion to God—God-consciousness. Peace and praise be upon them both.

A fourth characteristic that Jesus and Muhammad shared was respect for the equality of women. Both of them lived in a highly patriarchal culture in which women were highly subjugated, had few rights, and were often treated unjustly and harshly. In speaking out on behalf of the rights of women, Jesus and Muhammad went against the prevailing norms of their respective cultural and religious heritage. We see, for example, in the ways that Jesus related to women a teaching that was quite revolutionary for his time. He treated women with the respect and dignity that they deserved. It is a woman, Mary Magdalene, who is recognized as one of his closest followers, and it was she to whom Jesus first appeared after his resurrection, entrusting to her the task of telling the other disciples that he had risen from the dead. In Jesus' understanding of the Kingdom of God, men and women were equals.

The Prophet Muhammad also courageously opposed the prevailing norms of his time with regard to women. In the fourth chapter of the Qur'an, Allah reminds believers:

> "O mankind! Reverence your Guardian-lord, Who created you from a single Person, created, of like nature, his mate, and from them twain scattered (like seeds) countless men and women; reverence Allah, through Whom you demand your mutual (rights), and (reverence) the wombs (that bore you): for Allah ever watches over you. (Nisa 4:1)

In addition to this *ayat* from the Qur'an, there is a *hadith* in which Muhammad says that "women are the twin halves of men." These teachings taken together are compelling evidence of the essential equality that exists between men and women, as it was revealed to Muhammad. It is this recognition of equality that forms the basis for the various laws of the *Sharia* which protect the rights of women. There are, for example, laws that protect women's right of inheritance, their right to divorce, their right to vote and run for office, their rights to alimony and palimony, and strict laws limiting polygamy. Indeed, one of the principle reasons for the limited conditions under which polygamy could be practiced was the protection of the many widows and orphans that lived without a husband or father in the often violent society of 7th century Arabia.

Though Islam is often criticized as being oppressive to women, the fact is that the teaching and example of Prophet Muhammad demonstrate something quite the opposite. Muhammad, like Jesus, was very counter-cultural in championing the rights of women. Yet it has often been the followers of Muhammad and Jesus who have misunderstood or misrepresented the rightful roles of women in society and in their respective religions.

Certainly, there are other convergences that can be pointed out between the lives of these two great messengers of God, and certainly there are some differences. However, the four that we have mentioned—being the beloved of God, defenders of the poor, being devoted to prayer, and defenders of women's rights—serve to highlight how much Muhammad and Jesus have in common. They lived several centuries apart, though they emerged from the same part of the world. One cannot help but wonder and speculate that if they lived at the same time and knew each other how they would have responded to each other. It is surely a hypothetical question, but the evidence would seem to indicate that they would not have seen each other as rivals, but would rather have had nothing but the highest respect for one another. The famous Night of Ascent in which Muhammad was mystically transported to heaven (*laylat al-miraj*) bears remarkable resemblance to the gospel account of Jesus' Transfiguration, where he was joined by the prophets Abraham and Elijah. In Muhammad's ascension he was also joined by Jesus. What a beautiful image. What did they say to each other? It is a fascinating question to ponder.

It is not hard to imagine them being glad to see each other, embracing each other as friends, and becoming engaged in deep and genuine dialogue. Indeed, it is not hard to imagine Jesus and Muhammad as friends, linked by their love of God and their vision of a world characterized by justice, compassion, and equality—a world where people lived in awareness of and submission to God. They would have recognized each other as friends because they were friends of God. They would have the same hope and expectation for their followers. May we, their followers, learn from them.

Issues Raised in the Aftermath of
THE CARTOON OFFENSE

Sefik Hikmet Toprak

The offensive editorial cartoons published in a Danish newspaper started a controversy that eventually led to protests all around the world. However strange it may sound, the editors of the paper claimed that they desired to test the extent to which freedom of speech could be exercised in their country. The Muslim minority of Denmark, who was not satisfied by their explanation, demanded an unequivocal apology. An apology was extended by the paper long after the protests had spread to the global scale. Danish Muslims felt that the issue was not about freedom of the press, but was rather yet another expression of "Islamophobia" or "anti-Islamic prejudice" in Europe, a sentiment that was also shared by Muslims at large.

It is not the intention of this article to speculate on the true motivation behind the printing of the blasphemous cartoons that derided and insulted the blessed memory of Prophet Muhammad, peace be upon him. Rather this article is intended to provide the reader with succinct answers to some frequently asked questions that were raised in the aftermath of the event.

THE ANCIENT PRACTICE OF MOCKERY

It would be appropriate to point out first that mocking sacred religious figures is not a practice initiated by the Danish newspaper in question. Prophets of earlier generations were constantly targets of mockery and derision. The following verse from the Qur'an, for example, attests to this fact:

> Ah! Alas for those servants! Every time there has come to them
> a Messenger, they have but mocked him. (Yasin 36:30)

There are explicit Qur'anic references to the ridicule that certain individual prophets were exposed to, but this general verse should be enough to prove the assertion.

THE DERISION SUFFERED BY PROPHET MUHAMMAD

Prophet Muhammad, peace be upon him, was no exception. He became a subject of mockery in his time after he started to communicate the message revealed to him, as indicated in the following verse, as well as in many others:

> Whenever they see you, they take you for nothing but an object
> of jest, (saying): "Is this the one whom God has sent as a
> Messenger?" (Furqan 25:41)

For the pagans of Mecca, they thought that if the long-awaited prophet were to appear among them, then the notables of their tribes were more worthy to be chosen than the orphan of Abdulmuttalib, peace be upon him. The Prophet constantly had to endure similar ridicule and other hardships in his time.

He also suffered derision from the people of the scripture, as the Qur'an points out in a few verses. For example:

> (O Messenger!) Say: "O People of the Book! Is it not that you
> dislike us only because we believe in God and what has been
> sent down to us and what was sent down before, and because
> most of you are transgressors?" (Maidah 5:59)

By asking this question without providing the answer, the Qur'an leaves the answer to the conscience of the audience. Muslims believe in one god, Allah. The Aramaic and Hebrew names Eloah, Elah, Eloi, Elohim are also from the same root as the Arabic word Allah. Muslims believe in the messengership of all the holy figures cited in both the New and Old Testaments. Is the problem with the final message that Muslims believe in that it came after the others? But note - if one and a half billion Muslims hold Moses, Jesus, and

Mary, peace be upon them, dearer than their own lives, it is because of this last message.

IDOLATRY AND ICON-WORSHIPPING

Another common question that was brought up in the wake of the cartoon crisis was about the depiction of the Prophet. It should be mentioned that there are few authentic traditions that place some reservations on representative arts in general, and discourage making the images of living creatures.

In order to understand the wisdom behind these reservations, the following aspects of the methodology of Islamic jurisprudence should be remembered. A general principle stipulates that all acts are judged according to their consequences; if the consequences are evil and detrimental than the act is considered unlawful, otherwise it is lawful. Another principle states that anything that helps or leads to what is unlawful is also unlawful.

Islamic faith is based on pure monotheism, and Islam is very strict against the manifestations of polytheism and idolatry in any form. No one possesses perfect, infinite, or absolute divine attributes other than the Almighty Creator himself. However great they may be, the created do not have a share in the divine attributes of the Creator.

Prophets are no exception to this rule. Islam, therefore, takes necessary precautions to ensure that all ways that could lead to idolatry in the form of hero worshipping are not practiced in the religion.

The following quote from the works of a renowned twentieth century Islamic scholar, Bediüzzaman Said Nursi, summarizes this and the wisdom that lies behind the restrictions imposed on images.

> Just as the Qur'an forbids in a severe fashion the worship of idols, so too does it forbids the worship of forms, which is a sort of imitation of idol-worship. Yet civilization counts forms as one of its virtues, and desires to dispute the Qur'an on this matter. But forms, whether images or concrete, either embody tyranny, or embody hypocrisy, or embody lust; they excite lust and encourage man to oppression, hypocrisy, and licentiousness. (25th Word)

In summary, making images for educational and other lawful causes is permitted. If the image is made for the purposes of or may lead to idolatry, or if it encourages oppression, hypocrisy, or excites lust, then it is not permitted.

It should be stressed that such restrictions on representative arts are not specific to Islam. Several Biblical verses in Exodus and Deuteronomy, for example, forbid making images. In fact, the second of the Ten Commandments stipulates this.

Moreover, the explanations given above should be enough to make it clear that these restrictions were placed for a specific purpose and they do not, in any way, imply that Islam is an adversary to the arts. As a matter of fact, Islamic civilization has produced the finest works of art in architecture, calligraphy, decorative arts, music, etc. In this matter the reader is referred to the numerous references available on Islamic art.

CALLIGRAPHIC PORTRAITS OF THE MESSENGER

Muslim artists used calligraphy to depict a non-visual, thus acceptable, image of the Prophet. They have been commemorating his blessed legacy by depicting verbal images or "calligraphic portraits" of him. Such beautiful artwork that inscribes a description of the prophet in words is known as the *hilya al-saadat* and is very common, especially in Turkish calligraphy.

FREEDOM OF SPEECH

The protests in the Islamic world, notwithstanding the normative teachings of the Qur'an, may have given an impression that Islam gives little or no value to the freedom of expression. On the contrary, Islam holds that the attribute of speech is a valuable gift bestowed upon mankind as expressed in the following verse:

> The All-Merciful. He has taught the Qur'an (to humanity and, through them, to the jinn); He has created the human; He has taught him speech. (Rahman 55:1-4)

Man is the vicegerent of God on earth. Compared to the rest of creation, the divine attributes of God are manifested in the most perfect way in human beings. The sounds that an animal make can never be described as speech. In that sense, the attribute of speech and the freedom to exercise that power is what makes us truly human.

Numerous passages in the Qur'an, the eternal message of God, quote the words spoken by unbelievers. The objections and suspicions they raised are then refuted by Qur'anic evidence and truth. If nothing else, this alone should be enough to establish the significance of freedom of conviction and freedom of speech in Islam.

Every type of freedom is associated with a certain set of responsibilities and ethics that prevent its abuse. Freedom of speech, in particular, should be exercised with respect for all members of the society. Needless to say, ridicule, insults, and harassment do not fall into the category of freedom of expression.

Among several verses in the Qur'an that teach the ethics of speech, the following is related to the main topic of this article:

> O you who believe! Let not some men among you deride others, it may be that the latter are better than the former; nor let some women deride other women, it may be that the latter are better than the former. Nor defame one another and therefore your own selves, nor call one another by nicknames (which your brothers and sisters do not like). How evil is calling one by names that connote transgressions after one has embraced faith, and how evil it is thereby to be marked with transgression after being marked with faith. Whoever does not turn to God in repentance and give up doing so, such are indeed wrongdoers. (Hujurat 49:11)

GOOD REPELS EVIL

The Qur'an also teaches the errors that can be made in speech and the etiquette of responding to such errors. It is important to stress that the violence witnessed in the protests in Muslim countries that followed the publication of the cartoons in no way reflects the normative teachings of the Qur'an. Read, for example, the following verse:

The true servants of the All-Merciful are those who move and act on the Earth gently and humbly, and when the ignorant, foolish ones address and treat them (in a way that originates from their ignorance and foolishness), they simply continue, wishing peace on them. (Furqan 25:63)

As a general principle, the Qur'an teaches to repel evil with good and encourages forgiving others:

(But whatever they may say or do,) repel the evil (done to you and committed against your mission) with the best of what you can do. We are best aware of all which they falsely attribute to Us. (Muminun 23:96)

However, it should be noted that,

The recompense of an evil deed can only be an evil equal to it; but whoever pardons and makes reconciliation, his reward is due from God. Surely He does not love the wrongdoers. (Shura 42:40)

RESPONSES

Islamic scholars commented on the cartoon crises, denouncing the defamation perpetrated by the editors of the Danish paper as well as the protests that followed. The following excerpt is taken from a transcribed speech of a renowned Turkish scholar, Fethullah Gulen, who also serves as the honorary president of the Writers and Journalists Association based in Turkey.

Freedom of expression does not authorize anyone to defame others. There is certainly a freedom of disseminating one's thoughts, but if you do not take others' thoughts into consideration you will leave them with no freedom. There should be boundaries between freedoms.

Bigotry is present in every country and we have seen many examples. In the face of all this foolishness, we still should act upon reason. Our religion does not cause us to disregard other religions; (on the contrary) it causes us to feel respect toward them. Our religion encourages us to get together with everyone,

it desires that we open our doors to everyone, and we do open
our hearts to everyone. You must be respectful to everyone.[1]

The media is invariably seeking the sensational, and is reluc-
tant to tune in to the moderate voices. As a result, an incurious and
indifferent member of the audience is exposed to only one side of
the story. Contrary to the expected outcome of telecommunication
technology, on occasion the media serves as an agency of disinfor-
mation. It is therefore crucial for a world citizen to apply to multiple media outlets in order to attain a balanced view of events on a
global scale.

Another important scholar of Egyptian origin and the head of
the International Association of Muslim Scholars, Yusuf al-Qaradawi,
said:

> The sabotage done by some Muslims in some capitals in
> response to the offensive cartoons is unacceptable and should
> be denounced.

The final quote is taken from a joint statement issued by the
Secretary General of the Organization of Islamic Conference, Ekme-
leddin Ihsanoglu, and his colleagues:

> We fully uphold the right of free speech. But we understand the
> deep hurt and widespread indignation felt in the Muslim
> world. We believe freedom of the press entails responsibility
> and discretion, and should respect the beliefs and tenets of all
> religions. But we also believe the recent violent acts surpass the
> limits of peaceful protest.

THE UNIVERSAL MERCY

What could be more erroneous than depicting Prophet Muhammad—
God forbid the thought—as a supporter of violence or of terror?
Such a claim is nothing but an expression of strong prejudice and
hatred. In reality, he was the embodiment of mercy and compassion.

---

[1] http://en.fgulen.com/content/view/2179/14/

It is impossible to do justice to the compassionate disposition of the Prophet in a short article. Various biographies have devoted chapters in praising his merciful character and there are many books written specifically on this topic. The few traditions quoted below are included for the sake of completeness and are intended to give the uninformed reader a first impression. Anas bin Malik, who was honored in serving the Messenger for ten continuous years, said: "I've never seen a man who was more compassionate to his family members than Muhammad."[2] An insane woman pulled him by the hand and said: "Come with me and do my housework." He complied with her request.[3]

Such traditions clearly show that he was compassionate by nature and embraced his immediate family as well as other members of his community with abundant mercy.

The Battle of Uhud was a significant turning point in the history of Islam. God's Messenger was wounded on his blessed face and one of his teeth was broken. As many as seventy companions of the Prophet were killed in the battle. Among the martyrs was his noble uncle, Hamza, whose body was mutilated in revenge by Meccan unbelievers. All these severe circumstances did not prevent him from praying: "O God, forgive my people, for they do not know."[4]

Does this sound like a description of a man who would support violence and destruction? His mission was to save mankind, not to destroy it. His profound compassion was not restricted to his friends and companions, but was extended to his staunchest enemies. The next few examples show this to an even greater extent. He was full of mercy for all of creation. It is reported that he once said: "Pity those on earth so that those in the heavens will pity you."

We again hear from him that a prostitute was guided to the truth by God because she gave water to a dog dying of thirst. He noted that another woman was sent to Hell because she confined a cat without food and it subsequently died of hunger.

---

2   Muslim, *Fada'il*, 63.
3   Qadi Iyad, *al-Shifa*, 1:131, 133.
4   Muslim, *Jihad*, 101; Bukhari, *Anbiya*, 54.

Did not the Qur'an describe him as an embodiment of mercy? Read:

> We sent you not, but as a Mercy for all creatures. (Anbiya 21:107)

THE PROPHET'S MILITARY DIMENSION

It is, in general, not thought proper to describe Islam using restrictive terms. Statements like "Islam is a religion of peace," "Islam is a religion of reason," etc. reflect only certain aspects of the religion. However, it may be a comprehensive description to call Islam a religion of balance. Islam establishes a fine balance between the faith and good deed, between this world and the Hereafter, between the material and the spiritual, between the peace and use of force, etc.

Although this is not an article on the Islamic concept of peace and just war, it would be proper to contrast the use of force with universal mercy.

The Messenger Muhammad was a prophet who had to fight for his message and may be compared to previous prophets like Moses. Abraham, according to the Bible, also waged war against his enemies. It is permitted in Islam to take up arms under certain circumstances: in self defense, in defense of the oppressed and in defense of the freedom of conviction. The first verse revealed on this issue in the Qur'an stipulates:

> The believers against whom war is waged are given permission
> to fight in response, for they have been wronged. Surely, God
> has full power to help them to victory. (Hajj 22:39)

Conflict is a reality of social life, and it may not always be resolved in peaceful ways. Taking up arms to end injustice, for example, is an act of mercy shown for the oppressed. War is seen as an exception in Islam, a religion that gives the utmost value to human life, as explained in the following verse:

> He who kills a soul unless it be (in punishment) for murder or
> for causing unrest and spreading corruption on the Earth shall
> be (considered) as having killed all humankind; and he who

saves a life shall be as if he had saved the lives of all humankind. And, indeed, there came to them Our Messengers again and again with clear Revelations (to convey to them such directives so that they might be revived both individually and socially) and signs—miracles—(proving their Messengership). Yet, notwithstanding all this, many of them go on committing all kinds of excesses on the Earth. (Maidah 5:32)

Finally, it may be instructive to give a count of casualties in the battles of Prophet Muhammad. The chart below shows that the total number of casualties did not exceed 400 inthe entire 23 years of his lifetime as a prophet.

Engagement	Opposing force	Opposition casualties	Muslim force	Muslims casualties
Badr	950	70	313	14
Uhud	3,000	22	700	70
Khandaq	12,000	8	3,000	6
Khaibar	20,000	93	1,500	15
Mu'ta	100,000	Not Recorded	3,000	13
Hunain	Not Recorded	70	12,000	70
Taif	Not Recorded	Not Recorded	12,000	12

This supports the general principle of Islam that the use of force is allowed when it is absolutely necessary and to the extent that it is absolutely necessary. In contrast, it may also be instructive to remember the terrible atrocities perpetrated in the twentieth century all over the world, which have claimed the lives of millions and millions of innocent people.

BEAUTIFUL MINDS

It is true that anti-Islamic prejudice is more widespread in the West than it has ever been before. On the other hand, it is also true that many intellectuals, philosophers, members of the clergy, Eastern and Western alike, both in the past and in the present have voiced their opinions against such bigotry. Many have praised the prophetic and personal qualities of Prophet Muhammad emphatically. Here are few examples from the past:

Lamartine deemed it proper to ask, in his *Historie de la Turquie*, whether there was any man greater than Prophet Muhammad in regards to all the standards by which human greatness may be measured. Sir Bernard Shaw stated, in *The Genuine Islam*, that, in his opinion, Prophet Muhammad must be called the savior of humanity. Michael H. Hart, in *The 100*, stated that Prophet Muhammad's unparalleled combination of secular and religious influence entitled him to be considered the most influential single figure in human history.

Thomas Carlyle, in his *Heroes and Hero Worship* and *The Heroic in History*, grieved the lies heaped round Prophet Muhammad, and labeled them as a disgrace. Gandhi, in *Young India*, expressed his strong conviction that it was not the sword that conquered lands for Islam, but it was the Prophet's noble character that won hearts.

Indeed, millions of Muslims travel to Mecca every year to show their love and devotion to God and their gratitude and respect to the rose of their hearts, Prophet Muhammad. It was he who illuminated the lives of billions with the knowledge of God. It was he who taught his followers how to prosper both in this world and in the next. It was he who brought the message of universal mercy and it was he who lived up to it. It is incumbent on every person, whether Muslim or not, to learn more about the pride of mankind. May God shower His boundless mercy, peace, and blessings on him at all times.

It would be fit to conclude this article with the words of M. Fethullah Gülen:

> "If only mankind had known Muhammad, peace be upon him, they would have fallen in love with him, as Majnun fell in love with Layla. Whenever his name is mentioned, they would tremble with joy and their eyes would be filled with tears."

Some books are undeservedly forgotten;
none are undeservedly remembered.

W. H. Auden

THE STORY OF *TARIKH-I MUHAMMADIY*

AN EXEMPLARY WORK OF DEVOTION TO THE PROPHET

Interview with Kutlukhan Shakirov
by Tahir Taner

E very book has its own story. When the author types the final full stop, the relief can only be compared to the birth of a child. Only mothers can understand what an author suffers as they both share similar pangs of producing a new life. Carol Burnett describes the feeling concisely: "Words, once they are printed, have a life of their own." Putting the full stop took a bit longer for Kutlukhan Shakirov when giving birth to his father's *Tarikh-i Muhammadiy*. The following interview with Dr Shakirov presents the tragic story of his father's book that is devoted to teaching about the life of the Prophet Muhammad, peace and blessings be upon him, to a nation that was deprived of religious belief and practice for almost a century under a communist regime. The story of this book, its suppression, and its eventual liberation highlights the Prophet's centrality in the world of his followers. It also illustrates that even under the most dire of conditions, 1400 years of tradition can find light and the Prophet's story can find a voice.

Dr Shakirov is an associate professor of economics who lives in Istanbul with his family. He was born in Gulja, Eastern Turkistan, but raised in Tashkent, Uzbekistan. After completing his degree on economics at Tashkent University, he served in the Red Army. After working for long years at the Scientific Research Center under the Uzbek State Planning Organization, he taught at the Tashkent University of Economics 1988-1996. He prepared more than 60 papers and articles on economics and Central Asian history and languages.

*Could you tell us about your father, the author
of Tarikh-i Muhammadiy?*

My father, Alikhantura Saghuni, was born to an Uzbek family in
1885 in the city of Tokmak (formerly Balasagun) in what is today
Kyrgyzstan. He attended schools and madrasas in Mecca, Medina,
and Bukhara. He actively participated in the armed uprising of the
Turkistan peoples against the Tsarist Russia in 1914 and 1916. He
was the first scholar to denounce sending children to the Russian
army to fight against the Ottomans during the First World War.

He was incarcerated 6 times. He was the first president of the
Islamic Republic of Eastern Turkistan in 1945-1946. He also held the
title of Marshal, Commander-in-chief for the National Army. He participated in more than 300 military operations and fought for independence against China. He was later kidnapped to the Soviet Union,
an event which was concealed from the world. He authored *Tarikh-i
Muhammadiy* (The History of Muhammed), *Turkistan Kaygisi* (Turkistan Anxiety), *Shifa al-ilal* (Cure for Illnesses). Among his translations are *Tüzükat-i Timur* (Political and Military Institutes of Timour),
Musika Risalesi (The Epistle of Music) by Dervish Ali Cengi, *Navadir
al-vakayeh* (Rare Events) by Ahmet Danish, *Buhara or the History of
Mawarannahr* by Herman Vambery. Until the day he died in 1976 in
Tashkent, he strove with utmost effort for the preservation of Islamic
faith and our cultural heritage. After the independence of Uzbekistan,
his name was given to two mosques, a high school, and a residential
area as a tribute to his memory.

*Tell us about the circumstances in which Tarikh-i
Muhammadiy was written.*

The author mentions in the preface that the drafts were first turned
into a fair copy in 1960 (AH 1380) on the 26th of Ramadan. I esti-
mate that the book was written in 1957-58. That period was around
the 40th anniversary of the establishment of the Soviet Union, when
they started to challenge the world. The first satellite to space was
launched and Cuba was established with a communist regime right

next door to the USA. The uprisings in Poland and Hungary were suppressed with bloodshed and harsh administration reigned in Russia. The religious oppression, relaxed during the Second World War was reintroduced and tightened under Kruschev. The Communist Party already had a concrete goal: to uproot all religious faith, including Islam by 1980 and to establish an entirely atheist society. To this end, diverse schemes were planned and staff was employed to close down mosques, to minimize the number of practicing Muslims, and to discourage attendance to religious celebrations. In those days, to become an enemy of religion was paramount to a profession. Campaigns to fight "fundamentalism and superstition" were organized from time to time, and with this excuse our mosques, madrasas and all other cultural heritage were being destroyed. In our country, which used to be famous as "Samarqand saykali ruyi zamin est, Bukhara quwwati Islami diyn est" (Samarqand is the luster of the earth, Bukhara is the strength of Islam) the new motto minted was "Al-Islamu fil-libas, wa'l-Qur'anu fil-kitab" (Islam remains in clothing, and the Qur'an in its binding). At least two generations were brought up with atheism and hatred toward belief. At this time, my father wrote *Tarikh-i Muhammadiy* in secret. There was always a danger of being discovered and freedom of thought was banned. Roughly written manuscripts were made into fair copy in notebooks, which were later compiled in two volumes by my brother Muhammedyar, who had a good hand. These two volumes were taken as the blueprint for the mass printing which had to take place after 30 years of hiding the manuscripts.

My late father kept this work with him at all times. *Tarikh-i Muhammadiy* totaled more than 1,000 pages. We read it at our family gatherings and friendly circles every Thursday. The book was soon recognized by our community, which led my father to take extra care not to lose it. Since all copying machines and typewriters were under state control, my father commissioned a reliable calligrapher to make a second copy of the book; this did not continue as my father died in 1976.

My father wrote this book in the Chagatay Turkish language and in Arabic script which had been our national alphabet for 1,300 years. Unfortunately, not too many people were left who could read this script, as it had been replaced first with Latin in 1928 and then with Cyrillic in 1940. So, it was necessary to re-write the book in Cyrillic so that we could reach a broader readership. Our first attempts to this end were obstructed. My nephew, Necat, for instance, had to face oppression by Soviet police, and even if he was not punished, he received threats from them. So, we had to postpone re-writing it in Cyrillic.

After my father passed away, my brothers and I made an agreement: none of us would reveal information about where the book was; if asked about its existence, each of us would refer to another brother. I was to refer to my senior brother Asılhan. Before the funeral procession, a towering man with an intellectual look came to us and said that the Uzbek Academy of Sciences was interested in acquiring Alikhantura's *Tarikh-i Muhammadiy* manuscripts and his entire library. We immediately refused, saying that we were not pleased by such an "honor." How could we rely on a regime which threw our most precious books into rivers and buried them to destroy them? At that time I was the one who kept the book at my father's house. It sometimes felt as if I was keeping a bomb with me. Mixed with apprehension and fear, the dominant feeling we had was a consciousness of serving the faith and carrying out my father's will. It was not until much later that they discovered I had the book. Their considerably generous proposal was again rejected and after this second refusal we began to await coercion. I put the book and all the manuscripts in a tin box and buried it in one of the corners of our garden. Each rainfall was terrifying for me and I had to dig out the box at midnight after rainy days to check whether they had been soaked or not. I remember I sometimes hid the box under rice and flour bags too, that is, until Gorbachev declared glasnost and perestroika.

I cannot remember the date exactly, but one Spring day in 1988, I was asleep in our living room. I woke up to hear a crash;

the heavy frame of my father's picture had fallen off the wall to pierce the sofa, merely an inch away from my head. I took this as a sign to take action. From that day on I worked from midnight to 5-6 am for two years and re-wrote the copy of the book in Cyrillic from the drafts of my relative Yahyahan. The book was finally ready for printing, but my eyesight had been damaged in the meantime and I started wearing eyeglasses. My experience during this re-writing was that I never felt any tiredness or boredom; on the contrary every turn of the page and every new title added more to my pleasure and joy. My wife Merhametay was a great companion and assisted in the writing all throughout this process. I still think it was the most meaningful thing I have done in my entire life.

What about the content and some literary aspects of the book?

The title *Tarikh-i Muhammadiy* (The History of Muhammad) refers to a meaning as significant as concepts like *"haqiqat al-Muhammadi"* (the truth of Muhammad) or *"mujizat al-Ahmadi"* (the miracles of Ahmad). It is certainly within the category of *seerah*—the life of the Prophet. In the 1,400 year history of Islam there have been quite a number of works in Arabic, Persian, Turkish, and other languages of the world on the life of the Prophet. Alikhantura Saghuni's work is based upon the most respected works of such literature, while his commentaries after every topic present the accounts in a way that is more beneficial for the reader. An eloquent style of discourse is used as much as possible so that it is more appealing to a wider readership. Many have commented that the book is not to be read once like a novel. Frequent reference to the book provides guidance to the reader and allows them to discover new thoughts that consequently lead to unique implications. I believe this book is a must for scholars of religion and for those who seek knowledge. The importance of the book also lies in the fact that it was written in clear Turkish at those dark times when even uttering the word "Turk" would bring down punishment. The author says, "I have written the histories of our blessed Prophet Muhammad, peace and blessings be upon him, the wise Qur'an, and the Ka'ba in Turkish, my own language, for our future generations as a keepsake from me."

More importantly, the book is also evidence of how the scholars of Islam preserved their faith under conditions that were perhaps even worse than those during the Age of Ignorance (*jahilliya*), how they defended it from totalistic oppression. This book exemplifies how the love of Prophet was perceived and experienced by these scholars. Many religious-spiritual words like *"haq"* (rights), *"ilahi basharat"* (divine glad tidings), *"ahirat"* (hereafter), *"takdir-i ilahi"* (divine will), *"ruh"* (soul), *"rahmanilik"* (divinity), *"gayb"* (unseen/unperceived), that have been left to oblivion under the influence of the atheist regime in Turkistan, have been revived thanks to the existence of this book.

What were the challenges you had to face during the printing process?

We had to work as a competent team. I focused on editing while my nephew Bahmanyar and a friend Abdulbasit dealt with contacts and financial matters. The Soviet Union was still standing, therefore we had to ensure that our efforts were established legally, on firm ground. The circumstances in Uzbekistan did not enable us to do it there, so we made a contract with Bulak, an Estonian-American company in Estonia, which undertook clearance from official procedures like censorship-check in return for a fee. With the authority of this company and its branch in Tashkent, we had our book printed by a prestigious printer in Uzbekistan. Without making too much fuss about it and with no publicity, we printed approximately eighty thousand copies in the first print. We invested a lot in it and never had any thoughts of royalty or profit. When the blueprints were brought to me for the final check, I could not believe my eyes; I still had feelings of fear, as it would not surprise me that the regime would intervene even at that phase.

We loaded books onto a few trucks after printing. We urgently needed a warehouse; this is something that we had overlooked. I spoke with Bulak, indicating my house as the warehouse and myself as its keeper in the official papers. We stored the books in my garage and two rooms of my house; the wooden floor sank 10-15 cm.

My house served as the center for distribution of this book for booksellers; they came during the night and bought 100-200 copies at a low price (5 rubles). The price of the book rose to 80-100 rubles in a short time, but we could not stop pirating. Although at first we managed to stop them by showing them our copyright as the children of the author, our control over them did not last for long.

Not much later, the Uzbek State television channel broadcasted a show about the book during which they made an announcement to the viewers to contact them if they knew anything about the author's family. As our secret was already revealed we thought it was not worth hiding any longer.

Was there much interest in the book?

There was a lot of interest which proved to me how my nation had preserved its devotion to Islam and to the Prophet Muhammad, peace and blessings be upon him. In all three editions the total number of copies printed numbered more than 110 thousand. We received many letters of thanks, stating the appreciation of people for the book's contribution to religious learning and the truth of existence. A chemistry professor said he was studying this book every night with his biologist wife, and that it had come as a salvation in their search for the meaning of life. An imam wrote that he was giving lessons from this book every night after *isha* prayer in the mosque. A prisoner from Bukhara wrote on behalf of a group of inmates: "I am writing from this place where no one would ever want to stay. We had lost our hopes for this world and our life had no meaning. We have been revived after reading *Tarikh-i Muhammadiy*. We came to know God Almighty. We have 2-3 copies only, which have worn out, please send us at least 30 copies." Today, *Tarikh-i Muhammadiy* is a textbook in all madrasas in Uzbekistan, it is a course offered at Tashkent Islam University, and it is officially recommended as a source of reference for theological departments at other universities. Translations into world languages will soon be underway.

UNDERSTANDING THE PROPHET'S MESSAGE TODAY

Hasan Horkuc

In his message the Prophet Muhammad, peace and blessings be upon him, underlines two basic aims in the creation of this universe: The first is to make known all the varieties of the Creator's arts and abilities so that we may offer Him gratitude and worship. The second is to make known to us, by means of natural sciences, all the manifestations of the Divine attributes in the universe so that we may experience them. By recognizing the Divine through experiencing its manifestations, we will come to believe in them.[1]

Muslims believe that mankind came to this world to be perfected by means of knowledge. and through prayer that is based on "true" belief. Thus, human beings develop during their life on earth and are perfected through the achievement of these two basic aims. Through these, a person is able to become a "true human being."[2]

I believe it is important to point out that Islam, the message revealed to the Prophet Muhammad, was not a new message. In fact, it was a continuation of the Divine messages revealed previously. It was the "completion" and "perfection" of all Divine revelations. It is the Prophet Muhammad's message that makes God known to man, which is provided by the Messengership and Islam. "Messengership holds the testimony of the greatest consensus and most comprehensive agreement of all the prophets. Islam bears the spirit of Divine religions and their confirmation based on Revelation."[3]

---

[1] See and compare with Bediüzzaman Said Nursi, *The Words*, trans. Sukran Vahide (Istanbul: Sozler Nesriyat, 1992), 133-35.

[2] See ibid., 139.

[3] Said Nursi, *Epitomes of Light (Mathnawi al-Nuri): The Essentials of the Risale-i Nur*, trans. Ali Unal (Izmir: Kaynak, 1999), 439.

Although the Message itself is absolute, the understanding of the Message can vary. Such variation depends on variables like time and place, the way the Message has been delivered and/or the way that it has been received. Two individuals, each in a particular situation, can receive the Message, but understand it in two totally different ways. Despite this, the Message itself remains absolute. Even sacred laws change in different ages. Indeed, in the same age, different prophets may, and have, revealed the same core message, but with different emphases and different details. There have even been different prophets and laws on the same continent and in the same century.[4]

In other words we should be open to many different levels of understanding that reflect pluralism. This is not a relativist position, but rather we are emphasizing the importance of the role of the individual in interpretation. The Qur'anic prescription is not general, but absolute and, as such, can be restricted.

There is a great diversity and tolerance that we can derive from this message. According to the Message brought to us by the Prophet Muhammad, mankind is unique in its ability to manifest and reflect all of the Attributes of its Creator. However, each Attribute can be reflected in different degrees.[5]

This way of understanding the Message can be applied if we take into consideration the individual. One person has numerous roles, each of them displaying different qualities of their character, each representing different degrees of different manifestations of the attributes of the Creator. Hence, we accept diversity in understanding the Message in all areas of life, from religion to ethnicity, from moderation to salvation. This view is neither absolutist nor relativist.

Another example of how to understand the Islamic Message is illustrated in the following statement:

> Yet a man is not loved for himself. Maybe he is loved for his attributes or his action. It therefore doesn't necessarily mean

4 See and compare with Hasan Horkuc, "Said Nursi's Ideal for Human Society: Moral and Social Reform in the Risale-i Nur" (PhD, University of Durham, 2004), 167.

5 See and compare with Nursi, *The Words*, 343.

that all of the attributes and actions of a Muslim are Islamic and contrarily all of the attributes and actions of a non-Muslim are un-Islamic. Just as not all of the characteristics of an individual Muslim necessarily reflect the teachings of Islam, neither are all of the qualities of followers of other religions un-Islamic.[6]

This means that Islamic attributes and actions might easily be observed in non-Muslims. The Message for the Muslims is that if they find qualities that are in agreement with Islamic teachings in an individual, they should consider those qualities as praiseworthy, whatever this individual believes.[7] This is the basis for Islamic tolerance as well.

Believing that Islam is the middle way, we emphasize the importance of moderation and refraining from greed and excess by referring to the Prophet's saying: "Too much or too little of anything is not good. Moderation is the middle way."[8]

We accept different views, ideologies, and cultures. However, tolerance and diversity does not necessarily mean assimilation or conversion; rather these are essential ingredients for the smooth functioning of a multicultural world.

The Prophet's Message teaches us hope, love, and tolerance. In the words of an Islamic scholar: "The thing which is most worthy of love is love, and that most deserving of hatred is hatred itself. It is love that renders people's social life secure and that lead to happiness."[9] The days for hatred and hostility are numbered. In the words of Yunus Emre, a Sufi poet, "We should love the creation for the sake of its Creator."

---

[6] See as cited in Hasan Horkuc, "New Muslim Discourses on Pluralism in the Postmodern Age: Nursi on Religious Pluralism, and Tolerance," *American Journal of Islamic Social Sciences* 19, no. 2 (Spring, 2002): 76.

[7] See and compare with, passim, Horkuc, "Said Nursi's Ideal for Human Society: Moral and Social Reform in the Risale-i Nur", 167-68.

[8] See Bediüzzaman Said Nursi, *The Flashes*, trans. Sukran Vahide (Istanbul: Sozler Nesriyat, 1995), 43.

[9] As quoted in Horkuc, "New Muslim Discourses on Pluralism in the Postmodern Age: Nursi on Religious Pluralism, and Tolerance," 82.

PROPHET MUHAMMAD

(PEACE AND BLESSINGS BE UPON HIM)

Kerim Balcı

The Creator of this majestic universe wants to be known.

And because He wants to be known, He will make Himself known.

And because He will make Himself known, He will speak.

And because He will speak, He will speak with mankind who is conscious and intelligent.

And because He will speak with mankind, He will speak with the best and most salient of humans.

And then He will speak to all of mankind through that man, who will become his Messenger and Prophet.

Therefore, those who want to know the Creator of this majestic "palace of universe" must first find, listen, and follow the message of this Prophet.

What follows is an imaginary journey that we embark on to find that Blessed Guide.

What follows is an attempt to understand he who is known as the "Last Prophet"; a person who has had millions of followers over fifteen centuries; a person whose name is the Prophet Muhammad Mustafa, peace and blessings be upon him.

The Prophet Muhammad, whose truthfulness was testified by all who knew him, indicated the eloquent revelation of the Creator of the universe to prove his Prophethood. Those who look at this Qur'an, the index of the book of creation, will see how it speaks of the Messenger of its message:

> Muhammad is the Messenger of God, and the Last of the Prophets. (Ahzab 33:40)

> Muhammad is but a messenger, messengers (the like of whom) have passed away before him. (Al Imran 3:144)

> Surely We have revealed to you as We revealed to Noah, and the prophets after him, and We revealed to Abraham and Ishmael and Isaac and Jacob and the tribes, and Jesus and Job and Jonah and Aaron and Solomon, and as We imparted unto David the Psalms. (Nisa 4:163)

This Holy Book states that the Prophet Muhammad was sent *as a Mercy to the worlds* (Anbiya 21:107); that he was sent *as a bearer of good tidings and a warner* (Furqan 25:56 and Baqara 2:119); that he was *the first to believe* (An'am 6:14); that he called the people to believe in *God*, himself as *God's Messenger*, *the Book* that was revealed to him, and those *books that were revealed to messengers before Him* (Nisa 4:136).

This Miraculous Book does not deny the revelations that came before it; rather it testifies to their truthfulness and completes them (Baqara 2:41). It states that the Prophet Muhammad called those who believed in the prophets that came before him to the belief in one God (Al Imran 3:64).

And by relating, *To those who believe in God and His messengers and make no distinction between any of the messengers, we shall soon give their (due) rewards* (Nisa 4:152), the Prophet Muhammad taught that all prophets should be considered equal.

This Eternal Word of God not only demands belief in all prophets but also reminds us that the prophets of the past promised to believe in those that would come after them. It calls out to those who have been given a Book and Wisdom *be sure to believe in and help the prophet who confirms your scripture*. When everything in the skies and on the ground bows to the will of God in obedience and listens to Him, is it possible for us not to take heed of His call of faith? (Al Imran 3:81-83). Truly, we should say nothing but *We believe in God, and in what has been revealed to us and what was revealed to*

Abraham, Isma'il, Isaac, Jacob, and the Tribes, and in (the Books) given to Moses, Jesus, and the prophets, from their Lord: We make no distinction between one and another among them, and to God do we bow our will (in Islam) (Baqara 2:136).

This Great Book also speaks of the Prophet Muhammad's high station in God's regard:

> Muhammad, as one who invites to God's (grace) by His leave, and as a lamp spreading light. (Ahzab 33:46)

> And lo! You are of a tremendous character. (Qalam 68:4)

> Surely God and His angels bless the Prophet; O you who believe! Call for (Divine) blessings on him and salute him with a (becoming) salutation. (Ahzab 33:56)

> Say, (O Muhammad, to mankind): If you love God, follow me; God will love you and forgive you your sins. God is Forgiving, Merciful. (Al Imran 3:31)

Thus, we have seen from these Qur'anic verses that he who was known as "Muhammad The Trustworthy" was sincere and truthful when he claimed to be the Prophet of God. Now let us turn and listen to what he is saying. Let us hear what the prophet who holds the key to the meaning of the universe has to say about himself.

While on the one hand he shows his lofty station by saying that God calls him his Beloved, on the other hand he shows his humility and modesty by saying,

> "Do not exaggerate in your praise towards me. I am only God's messenger and servant."

On the one hand, he says "The first to be created was my light," on the other hand, he does not allow his followers to consider him greater than Prophet Jonah.

When speaking about the prophets that came before him he says, "I am the prayer of my ancestor Abraham and the good tidings of Prophet Jesus."

> My state and that of the other prophets is like the following
> parable: A man builds a perfect and beautiful house but leaves
> one brick missing from a corner of the house. People come and
> gaze at the house. Noticing the missing brick they say "Will a
> brick not be put in this niche?" Now, I am that brick and the
> last of the prophets.

He says that his true duty is to complete the exalted character.
He declares, "I am not the prophet of one tribe but the prophet of
the people of all colors." He says that love is the bond between
himself and the believers: "Love God for His bounties and love me
because of the love that God has for me."

What the Prophet wants is nothing more than love and a
greeting when mentioned.

Now, let us listen to what his believers say about him:

"His character is that of the Qur'an," said Aisha, his wife and
friend. His followers referred to him as a talking Qur'an. The Muslims
greeted him by singing when he arrived at Medina from Mecca:

> You are the moon, you are the sun,
> You are light upon light.
> You are the light of Surayya,[1]
> Oh Beloved, oh Messenger...

The expression of love for the Prophet is not restricted to the
narrations from his Companions. Poets spent entire lifetimes trying
to compose adequate lines and verses to duly state their love and
affection for the Prophet. Hassan Sabit said the following:

> I cannot extol the Prophet with my words; instead my men-
> tioning his name extols my words.

Imam Busri on the other hand expressed his admiration, saying,

> Even his miracles appear dim in comparison with his truth.

Rumi showed him as his source of inspiration:

---

[1] The Pleiades.

> I am a grain of sand on the path he treads.
> If anyone narrates anything from me but this,
> I am absolved of those words, and of him.

Yunus Emre expressed his yearning saying,

> I wish to discover the path that leads to you;
> I wish to immerse myself in the dust of that path.

Centuries later, Bediüzzaman Said Nursi said that it would be befitting to embroider a treatise about the Prophet with gold and diamonds. Beloveds of every age and century have called him the *Rose of Medina*, yearning for the death that would unite them with him.

This love and devotion towards the Prophet Muhammad is in itself testament to his truth. Since millions of people have turned towards him in love, respect, and adherence, we too will testify that Prophet Muhammad fulfilled his duty to the utmost degree.

THE MOST COMMONLY RECITED POEM IN THE WORLD:

THE MEVLIDI SHERIF

Ali Fuat Bilkan

D
o you know the poem recited more often, by more people, before more audiences, than any other in the world? It is Süleyman Çelebi's Mevlid (*Mawlid* in Arabic). Written in 1404, Çelebi's 800-couplet masterpiece is the crown of classical Turkish literature, and because of its focus on the essence and beauty of the Prophet, this piece of Turkish folklore has become a sacred treasure for Muslims around the world. It is not uncommon for Muslims to recite the Mevlid on occasions such as births, graduations, deaths, anniversaries, and the like. In this respect, the Mevlid is a work with no equal. Neither the work of Homer, La Fontaine, neither Baudelaire, Rimbaud, nor Shakespeare; Milton, Goethe, Pushkin, Poe, nor Dickenson has been recited as often times as the master work of Çelebi.

Since the tenth century, Muslim poets around the world have produced hundreds of poems in different languages dedicated to the blessed memory, message, and miracles of the Prophet. The fact that all these poems had the same themes led to developments in style, whereby one would influence the authorship of others. Undoubtedly, Süleyman Çelebi's Mevlid is primary in this respect. Since its initial recitation the Mevlid influenced Muslim poets around the world, and has been translated into many global languages, including a direct translation from Turkish to Arabic. (Bakirci, 2002: 116)

In English, Çelebi's Mevlid is known as the Mevlid-i Sherif, however, it remains largely unknown to the English-speaking world. F. Lyman MacCallum's English translation was first published in

1943 and then in 1957. MacCallum's work, however, was only a partial translation of the Mevlid; it consisted of a Prologue followed by the Fatiha (the first chapter of the Qur'an), a section on the Prophet's birth, his miracles, the Ascension, a supplication, a prayer, and a reprise of the Fatiha.

In the first ten pages, MacCallum discusses how the Turks kept the tradition of the Mevlid alive for five centuries. He provides the reader with a brief introduction to the poem, its history, as well as a short biography of Süleyman Çelebi. When discussing its authorship, MacCallum informs the reader of the Mevlid's first translation into a Western language, a German translation by Irmgard Engelke (Sulajman Tschelebi's Lobgedicht auf die Geburt des Propheten - Mevlid-i Şerif, Halle 1926), which was based on 360-630 couplets. MacCallum's work is derived from 263 couplets.

This text was published in Istanbul in 1931 (Süleyman Dede, *Mevlid-i Şerif*, Ahmet Halit Library, Istanbul, 1931). The author tells about the Mevlid ceremonies and some traditions observed at these ceremonies, finally giving the musical notes of the melody to which the Mevlid is sung.

This work, which introduced the world's most commonly recited poem to the world, is important in terms of objectively reflecting a society's religious sentiments. We hope such works that are ingrained in the culture of the people will help those who are curious about Islam to be able to understand the inner world of Muslims, and the love they cherish for the Prophet.

A few sample couplets from MacCallum's translation:
The Mevlidi Sherif

In the Name of God, the Merciful, the Compassionate
(Bismillahirrahmanirrahim)

Allah ! This name invoke we in the beginning,
For this is ever due from us, his servants
(Allah adın zikr edelim evvelâ / Vâcip oldur cümle işte her kula)

బ్ ౼

Allah ! The name which brings to all who call it,
God's present aid, the weight of labour light'ning.
(Allah adın her kim ol evvel ana / Her iki âsân ede Allah ana)

బ్ ౼

Were Allah's name to begin each fresh endeavour,
The end would ne'er fall short of full attainment.
(Allah adı olsa her işin önü / Hergiz ebter olmaya anın sonu)

బ్ ౼

With every breath repeat that name, unceasing;
In Allah's name see every task completed.
(Her nefesde Allah adın de müdam / Allah adıyla olur her iş tamam)

బ్ ౼

Salavat (Invoking blessings on the Prophet):

Blessing and greeting upon thee, O Apostle of Allah!
Blessing and greeting upon thee, O Beloved of Allah!

REFERENCES

- Hüseyin Vassâf. *Mevlid, Süleyman Çelebi ve Vesiletü'n-Necât'ı*, Haz.: Cemâl
- Kurnaz, Mustafa Tatçı, Akçağ Yay., Ankara: 1999.
- Selami Bakırcı. *Mevlid, Doğuşu ve Gelişmesi, Akademik Araştırmalar Yay.*, İstanbul: 2002.
- Süleyman Çelebi, *Vesiletü'n-Necât, Mevlid*, Haz.: Ahmet Ateş, TTK. Yay., 1954.
- Süleyman Çelebi. *Mevlid*, Haz.: Prof. Dr. Faruk Timurtaş, Kültür Bak. Yay. 3. bs., İstanbul: 1980.
- *The Mevlidi Sherif*, by Süleyman Çelebi, translated by F. Lyman MacCallum,
- John Murray Ltd. First published 1943, reprinted 1957.

THE PROPHET MUHAMMAD'S LOVE FOR CHILDREN

Yetkin Yildirim

T he heart of a child should be nurtured with belief in God and spirituality at an early age. Learning about God at an early age will help a child to overcome the difficulties of this life, not only in their childhood, but also in later adult years. The more a child is exposed to a community that observes religion, the easier it will be for that child to understand and accept religion and spirituality later in life. It has been observed that children who grow up in a spiritual environment are more likely to establish healthy relationships with their parents (Nursi 2002). Islam teaches that children are gifts from the all-compassionate and generous God. We should love and care for them with perfect compassion and tenderness so as to ensure their healthy growth.

The Prophet Muhammad, peace and blessings be upon him, whose wife Aisha referred to as the "Living Qur'an," exemplified the Islamic way of nurturing children's spirituality.

In many of his teachings, the Prophet Muhammad emphasized the importance of showing children kindness and compassion. Since children are weak and powerless, their spirits flourish best when they come to know and experience their compassionate and powerful Creator. Through trust in God and surrender to His guidance, children will be able to face fears and challenges throughout their life.

A child needs to feel safe, and the best way to give them this feeling is to teach them that God is the Most Merciful and the Most Compassionate and that He protects them from all evil. A child who is weak and needy can feel secure in life only through this belief. Furthermore, teaching a child to be grateful for everything they possess and receive is another vital aspect for healthy spiritual development. A child should be made aware that everything given to him or her ultimately comes from God. In this way, they will grow into a thankful and appreciative person.

Showing mercy and love to children has a special place in the Prophet Muhammad's teachings. When addressing the importance of mercy in spiritual development, the Prophet stated, "whoever does not show mercy to his children is not one of us [Muslims]." Thus the Prophet Muhammad taught that children should be approached with mercy, love, respect, and trust. His wife Aisha gave the following example:

> One day a person from the desert came to the Prophet Muhammad and said, "You are kissing children but traditionally we don't kiss them." The Prophet replied, "What can I do if God removed mercy from your heart?" (Bukhari, *Ahlaq*; Muslim, *Kitab al-Fadail*)

Another teaching by the Prophet on this concept concerns his grandson Hasan:

> One day the Prophet was in one of the markets of Medina. He left the market and so did I. Then he asked thrice, "Where is the small child?" Then he said, "Call Hasan." So Hasan got up and started walking with a necklace of beads around his neck. The Prophet stretched his hand out like this, and Hasan did the same. The Prophet embraced him and said, "O Allah! I love him, so please love him and love those who love him." Since Allah's Apostle said that, nothing has been dearer to me than Hasan. (Bukhari, *Libas*)

It is important to note, however, that the Prophet Muhammad was overall even-handed in his approach toward raising children. He was merciful and loving towards children, but he was also resolute in his guidance. Of the Prophet Muhammad, Fethullah Gülen (2000) notes the following:

The Messenger was completely balanced in the way he brought up his children. He loved his children and grandchildren very much, and instilled love in them. However, he never let his love for them be abused. None of them deliberately dared to do anything wrong. If they made an unintentional mistake, the Messenger's protection prevented them from going even slightly astray. He did this by wrapping them in love and an aura of dignity. For example, once Hasan or Hussein wanted to eat some of the dates that had been allocated for distribution among the poor as alms. The Messenger immediately took it from his hand, and said: "Anything given as alms is forbidden to us." In teaching them while they were young to be sensitive to forbidden acts, he established an important principle of education.

He never made any distinctions between his sons and daughters, saying "How beautiful a child is a girl—compassionate, helpful, easygoing, blessed, and full of motherly feelings." The Prophet Muhammad did not limit his love and mercy and showed love and mercy to children from different religions. He taught Muslims to treat neighbors of other faiths as their closest relatives. For example, the Prophet Muhammad visited one of his Jewish neighbor's sons when he was ill.

The Prophet Muhammad placed a special importance on playing with children. He encouraged parents to play with their children, and said that whoever has small children should become like children, too, in order to play with them. One time, the Prophet and some of his students were invited to a dinner. On the way to attend this dinner, they ran into the Prophet's grandson Hussein, who was a very young child. Hussein was playing with some other children when they saw him. When they saw the children, the Prophet Muhammad went forward and opened his arms wide in order to hug them, and the children started to run around in play. Then the Prophet Muhammad ran after Hussein to join him in his game until he caught him. When he caught Hussein, he put one hand under his chin and one hand at the back of his neck and kissed him.

Children are keen observers; they observe their surroundings closely, and their spiritual life is influenced by this. It is crucial to realize that the immediate family at home, the extended family, the environment at school, and friends all have an impact on the development of a child's spirituality. The Prophet Muhammad said that every child is born with an ability to become close to God, but that their environment might cause them to drift away.

Everything that surrounds a child has an effect on their soul. Therefore it is necessary that the environment to which the child is exposed should be chosen carefully. Islamic scholars state that the imperfections that a child may absorb from harmful environments put a black spot on their heart. For example, it is the spiritual obligation of all parents to protect their children from indecency and from people with immoral thoughts, licentious feelings, and sinful eyes. Keeping this in mind, the Prophet Muhammad stated that the first words that a child should hear should be *la ilaha illalah*, "There is no deity but God." A child's entire spiritual knowledge will be based on these first words.

According to Islam, spirituality enters life with daily religious practice. Prayer is one of the five main pillars in Islam. The Prophet Muhammad stated, "Prayer is the pillar that supports religion." Furthermore, the Prophet also stated that one experiences the closest proximity to God when prostrating in prayer. Thus we can understand that the highest level of spirituality is experienced through prayer. Therefore, praying with full concentration is important. To achieve this concentration, most people prefer a quiet atmosphere.

Even though the presence of children in places of worship may disturb people's concentration, the Prophet Muhammad did not remove children from places of prayer. It is reported that even if he was leading the congregational prayer, he did not insist that children leave the place of worship. The Prophet Muhammad went so far as to widen his stance so that children could pass through his legs in play while he led the prayer. Sometimes playing children climbed on his back while he was prostrating. In one case, a baby climbed on him while he was prostrated, and although he was leading the prayer, he remained in that position until the baby climbed down. The Prophet often shortened prayers so that mothers could take care of their babies' needs. The Prophet said, "When I stand for prayer, I intend to prolong it, but on hearing the cries of a child, I cut it short, as I dislike troubling the child's mother."

In some cases, he held babies in his arms to be able keep them in places of prayer while he was praying. He held them in his arms while he was standing and carefully placed them to his side when prostrating. On this issue the Prophet Muhammad did not make any distinction between boys and girls. It is reported that the Prophet Muhammad came to the mosque carrying Umamah, his granddaughter, on his shoulder. Keeping her on his shoulders, the Prophet Muhammad led [the people] in prayer. When he bowed, he put her down and took her up when he got up. He kept doing this until he finished his prayer.

Even while preaching the Prophet Muhammad did not seek to remove children from the congregation. One of his students said, "I saw our Prophet giving a sermon. Hasan was sitting on his knees. During his speech he occasionally would bow down, kiss the child, and say: "I love him."

We learn from these teachings that rather than remove children from places of worship, we should train ourselves to concentrate during prayer in the presence of children. This will improve our ability to focus on our relationship with God during prayer even in distracting environments. In Islam it is important to be able to live spiritually in all parts of life. This goal can be achieved by learning how to be with God even during the difficult times of our lives. A person who trains his concentration and spirit to be close to God during prayer, even in the presence of children, will be able to continue their spiritual focus during the difficult times of his life.

The Prophet Muhammad is a perfect example for how human beings can be elevated through the stations of spirituality. Following his example, Muslims are required to be transparent with their thoughts. In other words, a Muslim should not think one way and act differently. Thus, it is important to be consistent with children.

Witnessing an inconsistency between what adults say and do can lead to deep wounds in the spirituality of a child.

For example, a person might be spiritually healthy in all other respects, but if they are a miser, it might pollute their perfect spirit. Therefore, it is important to teach a child about sharing and having compassion for the needy and less fortunate. The suggested way of teaching is, again, through example; if parents show mercy towards the needy and share their wealth with them, a child will surely grasp the importance of this behavior.

If a parent wants their child to pray like them, they have to pray in the presence of the child in the most sincere and exemplary manner. Performing spiritually moving prayers in the presence of a child has a profound effect on them. Seeing their parent in a state of elation during a devout prayer can open a child's soul and may lead them to ask questions and learn about the prayer being performed. Explaining the spiritual delights of prayers and rituals in this state would naturally penetrate deeper into the soul of the child. Trying to explain the experience of a spiritually fulfilling ritual that one has never experienced would not have a similar effect on the child.

REFERENCES

- Darimi, Abu Muhammad Abdullah Abdurrahman. *Sunan*, Cagri Publications, Istanbul: 1992.

- Gülen, Fethullah.. *Prophet Muhammad: Aspects of his life*. Vol. 1. The Fountain, Virginia: 2000.

- Nursi, Said. *Existence and Divine Unity*, The Light Inc., NJ: 2002.

- Tabarani, Sulayman ibn Ahmad. *Al-Mu'jam al-kabir*. Wizarat al-Awqaf wa-al-Shu'un al-Diniyah, Baghdad: 1984.

- Tirmidhi, Muhammad Isa Sevre Musa. *Sunan*. Yunus Emre Publications, Istanbul: 1981.

THE UNIVERSAL MESSAGE
OF THE PROPHET

Zeki Saritoprak

Theologically speaking, the universality of the Prophet Muhammad's message, peace and blessings be upon him, comes from the concept of one God who is the God of all, not only the God of Muslims. God describes Himself in the first chapter of the Qur'an, which is recited by all Muslims around the world in their five daily prayers; He is the God of all creation, *"Rabb al-Alamin."* Whether humans are aware of this fact or not, God is the God of all mankind—Muslims, Christians, atheists, etc.—regardless of their differences. God is the creator of everything, with no exception. The Qur'an declares that a gigantic star and an atom are shoulder to shoulder, worshipping the same God; a fly and an elephant are brothers and sisters; all of creation is here to help us understand the meaning and the mystery of the universe.

Before addressing the universality of the Prophet Muhammad's message, it is essential to focus our attention to the era when Muhammad's message first emerged: fifteen hundred years ago in pre-Islamic Arabia. Although there were some positive characteristics of Arabs before Islam, such as generosity, courage, and dignity, the feudal system of society was so harsh that the marginalized did not have any rights. Slaves were persecuted, women were sold like property, and female infants in many cases were buried alive as a part of traditional tribal honor. Wars between tribes occurred uncontrollably. People worshipped idols and made their own gods according to their own desires.

Muhammad was born in 571 AD on the twelfth day of *Rabi al-Awaal* (the third month of the Arabic calendar). He came into this world in a time of ignorance and chaos. Throughout his adulthood he was not satisfied with the tribal traditions of his society. He would go into seclusion to meditate for long periods of time, particularly for the whole month of Ramadan. In the year 610 CE, he experienced his first revelation, an event that changed him and transformed the world forever. For twenty-three years thereafter, Muhammad received more revelations which were ultimately compiled as the Qur'an (recitation), the Holy Scripture of Islam. In a very short period of time, despite hostile reaction to his message, the Prophet's kindness and tenderness made an impact on the hearts of many in the city of Mecca.

The Prophet Muhammad did not consider himself a deity or a part of God, rather he saw himself as the messenger of God who was to convey God's message to the world. The Qur'an speaks of many prophets, like Abraham, Moses, John the Baptist, and Jesus. We have chapters in the Qur'an named after some of these prophets. There are also particular verses about the personality of the Prophet of Islam. In one verse the Qur'an speaks of him as *"rahmatan lil alamin,"* the mercy for many realms and worlds. Islamic scholars ask us to think, in order to understand the meaning of being merciful to creation, of the oppression that defined the world into which Muhammad was born, and the transformation that Muhammad's message caused.

Although the message of Muhammad addressed Arabs first, its nearest audience, it did not limit the message to the nation of Arabs, or for that matter to any nation. Many Qur'anic verses transcend locality, region, ethnicity, and nationality by starting with the call, "O Human beings," or, "O People."

The Prophet's message brings the idea that everything in creation is a living, chanting, obedient worshipper of God, regardless of whether they are humans, animals, or other creatures. Bediüzzaman Said Nursi speaks of one Qur'anic verse which says, "Everything in the heavens and earth praises God, although you may not understand their praise," (Isra 17:44) inviting the reader to enter the world in which the Qur'an was revealed and see the darkness that dominated it. In Arabia, before the Prophet, the meaning of creatures was not recognized. The Qur'anic revelation breathed life into the world: it taught those who would listen nature's splendor is not meaningless. According to the Qur'an, all things, human and non-human alike, praise God with great joy. Explaining this reality, Nursi invites his audience to ride the vehicle of history, to travel to the land of Arabia to see the situation there before and after the emergence of Islam. One should keep in mind that to change a little vice, such as a bad habit, is difficult enough, let alone changing the minds and the hearts of an entire society. According to Nursi, if 100 modern day philosophers with all their knowledge were to go to Arabia and work for 100 years, they would not be able to make the changes that Muhammad made in twenty-three years. He successfully transformed this wild society into a civilized community and shaped its leaders to construct a new civilization.[1]

If one would like to see the power of transformation that Muhammad made, one needs only to look at Umar, the second caliph: Umar before Islam and Umar after Islam. Umar himself said that he remembered two things from his pre-Islamic life: one, he would cry, and two, he would laugh. He cried that he buried his own daughter alive and he was still hearing her voice calling to him. He laughed that he made gods of flour which people ate when they were hungry. The new Umar became a symbol of justice for the world. Umar after Islam, during his caliphate, is known for the following statement: "if a wolf attacks a lamb at the shore of the Euphrates, I am afraid that God would ask me why I did not protect the lamb against the wolf." Out of compassion, he would walk among houses at night and see if there were some that needed food and he would anonymously feed those people. It was the universal message of Muhammad that transformed Umar into such an example of humanity.

Mercy and compassion constitute the foundation of the Prophet's message. In the *Basmala,* the statement that precedes the 113 chap-

---

[1]   For details of this comparison, see Bediüzzaman Said Nursi, *The Words*, trans. Şukran Vahide, Istanbul: Sözler Neşriyat, pp. 243-252.

ters of the Qur'an, God is described as having two attributes, the "Most Merciful and the Most Compassionate." This very statement has become the symbol of Islam. The Qur'anic verse says, "Muhammad, We have sent you as a mercy for all creation [*rahmatan lil alamin*]" (Anbiya 21:10). Being merciful towards all creation, Muhammad's personal life has become a reflection of this Qur'anic verse. In his relationships with people, he always smiled and no one ever heard a bad word from his mouth. In his family life, he showed the same mercy to his wives. His companion Anas ibn Malik, who faithfully served him for 13 years, witnessed this mercy, saying that he never received any reprimand for his service, despite his mistakes.

The Prophet was also very sensitive towards human suffering. When he heard of a slave being tortured, he commanded one of his companions to buy that slave's freedom. His famous hadith about the treatment of slaves is a great example of his universal teaching. He used to say, "They are your brothers; give them to eat what you eat, and give them to wear what you wear." Slaves demonstrated great love toward Muhammad. On one occasion, he asked Zaid Ibn Haritha, a slave freed by Muhammad, if he would like to go back to his family, but he chose not to go with his father who had come to take him, instead preferring to stay with the Prophet.

His farewell sermon on the plain of Arafat also has remarkable aspects of the universality of his message. In this sermon, he speaks about women, the relationship between races, and slaves. About slaves he says, "Fear Allah with regard to your slaves." Within thirty years after his death, it was difficult to find one slave in Arabia. The Qur'anic verse clearly says that "O people, We have created you from male and female and made you into nations and tribes to know one another. The best of you is the best in conduct" (Hujurat 49:13). In his last sermon the Prophet said that all humankind is from Adam and Eve: an Arab has no superiority over a non-Arab and a non-Arab has no superiority over an Arab. Also, a white person has no superiority over a black person and a black person has no superiority over a white person. Of women he said, "It is true that you have certain rights in regard to your women, but they also have rights over you." The Prophet successfully established a sense of responsibility and conscience in the minds and hearts of his people.

The Prophet's universal message of mercy did not include only human beings, but also animals. Among the miracles narrated in the collections of hadith, there is the story of a camel that came to Muhammad, prostrated itself before him as if saluting him, and spoke to him. According to certain other narrations, this camel had gone wild and would attack all who came near it. When the Prophet appeared, it came to him, prostrated itself as a sign of respect, and knelt beside him, allowing Muhammad to put on its bridle. Then the camel complained to the Prophet, "They have employed me in the heaviest work and now they want to slaughter me." Muhammad asked its owner, "Is it true?" "Yes," he said. Muhammad said to his companions, "These animals are communities like you. Be compassionate towards them." With regard to someone who overworked his donkey, the Prophet said, "Don't make the backs of your animals chairs." On another occasion, the Prophet saw a donkey on the road with a brand on its face, and said, "Allah's curse is on him who branded it."

The Prophet's mercy even extended to his enemies—he never sought revenge. It is reported in the hadith collection that at the battle of Ghatfan and Anmar the courageous head of a tribe named Ghuras slyly approached the Prophet and holding his sword over the Prophet's head asked, "Who will save you from me?" Muhammad replied, "Allah!" and prayed, "O Allah, suffice me against him." In the same breath, Ghuras was knocked down by a mysterious blow he received between his shoulders and his sword slipped out of his hand. The Prophet took the sword and asked him, "Now who will save you from me?" But the Prophet forgave him and allowed him to return to his tribe. His people were all surprised that such a courageous man had not been able to do anything against the Prophet. They asked, "What happened to you, why couldn't you do anything?" He told them what had happened, and added, "I am now coming from the presence of the best of men." In a fashion similar to this event, at the battle of Badr, a hypocrite from among his own men approached Muhammad. He had just lifted his sword when Muhammad turned and glanced at him, causing him to tremble and drop the sword. The Prophet again did not take revenge.

As the famous Muslim poet and mystic, Rumi, wrote:

> The light of Muhammad has become distributed in millions of pieces
> And has encompassed the whole world.
> The Prophet was like the lightening of that light.
> When it strikes, all veils of disbelief are torn and
> Thousands of monks are influenced by Muhammad and run toward him.
> ...
>
> His Words are all pearls from the ocean of reality
> Because his heart was united with the ocean of truth.

PROPHET MUHAMMAD AS A FRIEND OF THE ENVIRONMENT

Ahmet Işık

O ver the last several decades, the most industrialized countries have spent much time and energy discussing solutions to environmental issues. These issues include nuclear pollution, global warming, acid rain, ozone depletion, greenhouse effects, widespread toxic chemicals, and deforestation. Curiously, these developed countries possess only one forth of the world's population; and yet they produce and consume 80% of the world's GDP (gross domestic product). That is, by using natural resources faster than they can be replenished, these countries are more at fault in regard to environmental pollution. Contrary to underdeveloped countries, industrialized countries also have nuclear power plants and nuclear research facilities, and develop a variety of nuclear weapons, which causes more nuclear pollution since they do not have well planned environmental protection policies.

Many organizations such as Greenpeace, World Wildlife Fund, Friends of Earth, and United Nations Environmental Program were established to counteract the effects of environmental problems. In addition to these organizations, many countries have signed environmentally related protocols to achieve the same goal. No attempts, however, have resulted in fundamental solutions to the problems. This is largely the result if the fact that most industrialized countries do not obey the rules they agree upon and thus they put the planet's future in even greater danger. For example, underwritten in 1997 by 84 countries, the Kyoto Protocol was a draft agreement that committed its member nations to reduce their overall emissions of greenhouse gases. The most developed countries of the Kyoto Protocol are not implementing their promised reduction of gases.

Since religion provides people with a good standard of life and enlightens followers about problems faced in all aspects of life, religion also has the capacity to offer holistic solutions to environmental problems. It is the followers' job to retrieve the message from this holistic approach. Surely, all religions somehow encourage participants not to cause or to avoid those problems. In Islam, the conservation of the environment is based on the principle that all individual components of the environment were created by God, and that all living things were created by the Almighty Creator. Although the various components of the natural environment serve humanity as one of their functions, this does not imply that the only reason for their creation is to be used by mankind. Therefore, all living things in the environment deserve respect and protection. Prophet Muhammad, peace be upon him, was a great person in all aspects and he is the teacher of Islam and his life and actions are the most important guides to find the solutions to the problems of the modern life. As he guided Muslims toward the solutions to many problems, he also provided many examples about how to protect the natural resources and environment.

During the time of the Prophet, of course, there were no environmental problems like those that we deal with today. However, this does not mean that his ideas and actions are not readily available to be applied to modern day ecology, environmental awareness, sustainability, and related concerns about protection of the natural world. If his sayings and significant events in his life are closely examined, it can be seen that the Prophet was an advocate of environmental protection. Some people may even indicate this with the word "environmentalist," as he always advised his followers to work toward the conservation of the nature. He also tried to maintain a harmony between life and the nature. One saying of the Prophet mentions the importance and moral aspect of planting trees:

> There is none amongst the believers who plants a tree, or sows
> a seed, and then a bird, or a person, or an animal eats thereof,

but it is regarded as having given a charitable gift [for which there is great recompense]." (Bukhari, III:513)

Prophet Muhammad, peace be upon him, also favored the proper use of natural resources such as land and water, the sustainable production of livestock, and he advocated for great care when treating wounded and sick animals. Issues such as animal rights and environmental protection are being still discussed today as unresolved topics of intellectual panels and conferences. When Mecca was taken, not only did the Prophet instruct Muslims not to harm innocent people such as children and women, he also advised them not to cut the trees.

THE HUMAN ROLE IN PRESERVING THE NATURAL WORLD

Mankind is chosen as the caliph (vicegerent) of God because of its ability to think and reason. On earth all the resources are given to his service. Nature is created in balance, and as a steward of God, the human responsibility is to ensure that our actions do not disrupt this balance. While using natural resources like animals, plants, lands, forests, watercourses, we are also responsible for their protection. Stewardship does not imply superiority over other living beings: ownership belongs to God alone. All creatures, living or nonliving, have rights; but only mankind has the privilege to use them and to take advantage of them in a proper way. Nature is also the fundamental source of knowledge in Islam. Man can detect the signs of God in natural phenomena such as the succession of day and night, the water descent from the sky, and being a source of life on the earth, the winds, etc. Man has to observe and protect nature so as to better understand God.

SOME ACTIVITIES OF THE PROPHET CONCERNING ENVIRONMENTAL PROTECTION

Prophet Muhammad had a special interest in the nature of the human and natural environment. He always advised to live in harmony with the Creator and His creatures. His actions illustrated how to maintain a livable environment in terms of physical and moral values. One of the actions that he always performed and advised to his followers was planting trees. Once he planted 500 date trees. He reforested an area called Zurayb and that area was re-named "al-Ghaba," the forested area. Some of the hadiths, advise to plant trees whenever possible, Examples are as follows:

> When doomsday comes, if someone has a palm shoot in his hands, he should plant it. (Ibn Hanbal, III, 184, 191)

This suggests that even when hope is lost, planting should continue with us or without us. It is because of the fact that planting is good and it has a productive aspect. The action is not for the good of the person; planting trees is for others.

> Whoever plants a tree and diligently looks after it until it matures and bears fruit is rewarded. (Ibn Hanbal, V, 415)

The Prophet not only encouraged the sustainable use of fertile lands, he also told his followers about the benefits of converting unused land into productive areas: planting a tree, sowing a seed, and irrigating dry land were all regarded as charitable deeds according to the Prophet's sayings: "Whoever brings dead land to life, that is, cultivates wasteland, for him is a reward therein" (Bukhari, Muslim). Thus any person who irrigates a plot of "dead," or desert land becomes its rightful owner.

> As long as people and animals benefit from that fertilized area, the person would be accounted as committing charity. (Munawi, VI, 39)

> If a Muslim plants a tree or sows a field and men and beasts and birds eat from it, all of it is charity on his part. (Bukhari, VI, 122)

The Qur'an reads, *Do you not observe that God sends down rain from the sky, so that in the morning the earth becomes green?* (Hajj 22:63).

Consequently, some people see the color green as the most blessed of all colors for Muslims.

According to the Prophet, the earth is in service of mankind, but it should not be overexploited, polluted, or abused. Like all living things, land has rights. In order to protect land, forests, and wildlife, the Prophet declared some parts of the country to be special zones, or sanctuaries, known as *hima* and *haram*, in which resources such as trees and rivers were to be left untouched. Both are still in use today: *haram* areas are often around wells and water sources to protect the groundwater from being overused. *Hima* are particularly important to wildlife and forestry and usually designates an area of land where grazing, hunting, and woodcutting are restricted, or where certain animal species are protected. *Hima* and *haram* zones are similar to national or state parks or modern wildlife reservations we have in many countries today.

Medina and Taif were the most important ones of the *hima* and *haram* lands. Medina and the area surrounding it within a radius of 32 km were declared a protected area at the time of Prophet Muhammad. Cutting of trees was forbidden in that area (Bukhari, II, 220).

ANIMALS ALSO DESERVE RESPECT

"If anyone wrongfully kills even a sparrow, let alone anything greater, he will face God's interrogation" (Mishkat al-Masabih). These words reflect the great respect and love that the Prophet always showed towards animals. He believed that as part of God's creation, animals should be treated with dignity, and the hadith contains a large collection of traditions and stories about his relationship with animals. The hadiths show that he had particular consideration for horses and camels.

The Prophet instructs the followers to treat animals gently, to show them compassion, sympathy, and mercy. He asks his followers not to torture animals, not to overload them, and to take good care of them, and to use them in the proper ways. He was once asked whether there would be a reward for those who showed charity to nature and animals. He replied, "For charity shown to each creature with an open heart, there is a reward." He also said, "he who is kind and merciful towards animals, God will be kind and merciful towards him." Even in slaughtering animals, the Prophet showed great gentleness and sensitivity. While he did not practice vegetarianism, the hadiths clearly show that the Prophet was extremely sensitive to the suffering of animals, almost as though he shared their pain viscerally. Thus he recommends using sharp knives and a good method so that the animal can die quickly with as little pain as possible. He also warned against slaughtering an animal in the presence of other animals, or letting the animal witness the sharpening of blades, which to him was equal to "slaughtering the animal twice," a practice the Prophet condemned as "abominable." Therefore, animals must be cared for with utmost beneficence and compassion and we must strive to ensure the preservation of different species,

The Prophet was thoughtful also about the babies of the animals. Once he told a dairy farmer to allocate some of the milk for the baby of the goat he was milking. Also, hunting just for fun was not welcomed by the Prophet. He asked people not to take away the eggs and the babies of the birds and not to destruct their nests (Abu Dawud, III, 469).

Prophet Muhammad, peace be upon him, advised constructing at most two-story houses and buildings with a large backyard or garden. Some sources indicate that he had some tall buildings ruined (Kattani, II, 41-42).

USING WATER EFFECTIVELY

The miracle of water is emphasized in a particular verse where God, addressing those who may doubt the truth of resurrection, first gives the example of the growth of the fetus within the mother's womb, leading to the birth of a human being. The verse then concludes, *If you are still in doubt as to resurrection, consider this: you can*

*see the earth dry and lifeless and suddenly when we send down waters
upon it, it stirs and swells and puts forth every kind of lovely plant!* (Hajj
22:5)

In the desert where the Prophet lived, water was very important to maintain daily life. In this respect, water, the source of all
life on earth as is testified in the Qur'an, was a gift from God. *We
made from water every living thing* (Anbiya 21:30). The Qur'an constantly reminds believers that they are the guardians of God's creation on earth: *Consider the water which you drink. Was it you that
brought it down from the rain cloud or We? If We had pleased, We could
make it bitter* (Waqia 56:68-70).

Islam forbids wasting water, or using it without any benefit.
The preservation of water for the drinking of mankind, animal life,
bird life, and vegetation is a form of worship that gains the pleasure of God.

Using water efficiently and safeguarding its purity were two
important issues for the Prophet. We have seen that his concern about
the sustainable use of water led to the creation of *haram* zones in
the vicinity of water sources. But even when water was abundant,
he recommended that believers perform ablution by using water
thriftily, regardless of its source. The Prophet also warned against
water pollution by forbidding urination in stagnant water.

CONCLUSION

Prophet Muhammad's perception of nature and human, and of the
nature-human relationship gives the Muslim community a good
vision of environmental awareness. As the effects of environmental
problems in human life become profound, we will be more in need
of Prophet Muhammad's environmental view. In this context, the
challenge facing Muslim scholars and scientists is to formulate environmental issues such as deforestation, erosion, drought, flood, greenhouse effects, acid rain, nuclear power, genetic engineering, population growth, ad general sustainability on the basis of Qur'anic teachings, and on the actions and sayings of the Prophet Muhammad.

REFERENCES

- İbrahim Sarıçam, *Hz. Muhammed ve Evrensel Mesajı* (The Prophet Muhammad and His Universal Message), Directorate of Religious Affairs of Turkey, Ankara: 2002.
- Francesca De Chatel, "Prophet Muhammad Pioneer of Environmentalism,"http://www.islamicvoice.com/august.2003/opinion.htm
- United Nations Environment Programme, http://www.unep.org/I
- Frederick M. Denny, "Islam and Ecology: A Bestowed Trust, Inviting Balanced Stewardship," University of Colorado. http://environment.harvard.edu/religion/religion/islam/index.html
- Hasan Zillur Rahim, "Ecology in Islam: Protection of the Web of Life a Duty for Muslims," October 1991, p. 65, Understanding Islam.http://www.washington-report.org/backissues/1091/9110065.htm

HILYA AL-NABAWI

CALLIGRAPHIC PORTRAYAL OF THE PROPHET

Zühdü Mercan

Hilya, or "adornment," is a calligraphic portrayal of the Prophet according to a traditional Arabic account of his physical appearance. Alongside a physical description of the Prophet, a hilya consists of impressions of his character and his charismatic personality; eulogies and praise of the Prophet are customarily added to this account. Since the Islamic tradition abstains from illustrating the beloved Prophet, hilyas as verbal descriptions ornamented with the best works of calligraphy and illumination, have been preferred as samples of exquisite taste of believers' profound love for him.

According to a saying of the Prophet, "For him who sees my hilya after my death it is as if he had seen me myself, and he who sees it, longing for me, for him God will make Hellfire prohibited, and he will not be resurrected naked at Doomsday." In the Ottoman tradition with exceptional efforts by artists and scholars this hadith materialized into a special form of art.

Hilya al-Nabawi is believed to be means of divine blessings and protection from natural disasters and fire. Those who read them are believed that they might see the Prophet in their dreams and to have the good fortune to witness the Prophet as intercessor before God on the Day of Judgment. Therefore, Hilya al-Nabawi is greatly respected and positioned in the best corner of houses, shops, mosques, and palaces. First written in *naskhi* script, which was small in size so as to fit into one's pocket, the Hilya al-Nabawi was later transformed to panel form. Attributed to the seventeenth century Ottoman calligrapher Hafiz Osman, the panel form quickly became a significant part of the calligrapher's catalog. It has since become a common practice for students mastering calligraphy to compose a hilya when they are ready to receive the *ijazat* (diploma).

The text is most commonly based upon the narration of Ali, the Prophet's son-in-law, who was always in his company. There are other narrations from his adopted son Hind Ibn Abi Hala, Umm Ma'bad, and Abu Hurayra.

Although there are hundreds of different hilyas with respect to their writing styles and placement of texts, the composition of a hilya usually consists of the following parts:

1. Top section 2. Upper text circular area 3. Crescent. 4. Abu Bakr. 5. Umar, 6. Uthman, 7. Ali. 8. Middle section (usually the verse Anbiya 21:107). 9. Lower text. 10-11. Arms, 12. Inner frame. 13. Exterior frame.

In the name of God, the Merciful, the Compassionate

Ali ibn Talib describes the Messenger of Allah as follows:

"He was neither very tall (not so tall as to look down upon others), nor very short (not so short as to be looked down upon); he was of medium height, slightly over the average. His hair was not short or curly, nor was it straight; it was slightly wavy and tidy. His cheeks were not chubby, nor were they too slim or sunken to expose the bones of his face; his blessed face was slightly rounded and the color of his skin was white with a tint of red. His pupils were black and eyelashes were long. He had a well-built body, strong bones, and wide shoulders. He had a thin line of body hair in the middle of his chest that reached down to his

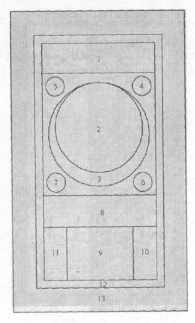

stomach. His hands and feet were of the perfect size. When he walked, he would lean forward as if walking downhill. When he turned his face, he would turn with his entire body. Between his shoulders he had the seal of prophethood, showing he was the last of the prophets.

We have only sent you as a mercy to the worlds. (Anbiya 21:107)

He was the most generous-hearted of people, the most eloquent in speech, and the softest in temperament. He knew the best manners (and had perfect relationships with others). Seeing him at a distance one would quiver and be filled with a sense of awe at his grandeur. However, once one was honored to become acquainted with him, he would love and feel nearness to him more than anything else. When describing him people would often claim, "I have not seen the like of him, neither before, nor after" in expression of their admiration.

THE FAREWELL SERMON OF THE PROPHET MUHAMMAD

PEACE AND BLESSINGS BE UPON HIM

The Farewell Sermon is a compilation of several sermons which were delivered at different times in Mina, Muzdalifa, and Arafat during the Prophet's pilgrimage in AH 10 (631). The Prophet addressed more than 100,000 believers who were observing the hajj, the major pilgrimage to the sacred precincts in Mecca. The hajj is one of the five pillars of Islam which is obligatory for those who can afford, at least once a lifetime.

The Prophet delivered his sermon in different locations and heralds repeated his words to the great number of people who attended. This sermon was called the "Farewell" Sermon because in this sermon the Prophet implied that he would soon die and that he would not be able to perform the pilgrimage another time. The days-to-come bore out this prediction and he was reunited with his Beloved within three months of the final sermon.

Several authentic hadith sources, such as Bukhari and Muslim, and translations by Muhammad Hamidullah and Nuh Ha Mim Keller have been used as references in compiling the following version of the sermon. Since the sermon was reported by different individuals, there are several versions in existence. There are minor differences but the essence is te same. Our goal in the current edition is to present the reader with the most comprehensive, authentic version as it can be derived from hadith sources.

In the Name of God,
the Most Compassionate, the Most Merciful

"All praise is due to God. We praise him, seek his help, ask his forgiveness, and we repent unto Him. We seek refuge in God from the evils of our selves and our bad actions. Whomever God guides none can lead astray, and whomever He leads astray has none to guide him. I testify that there is no deity but God alone, without any partner and I testify that Muhammad is His servant and messenger. I enjoin you, O servants of God, to be pious toward God, I urge you to obey Him, and I begin with that which is best.

❧

"O people,
listen to me well, for I do not know if I will be amongst you again after this year. Therefore, listen to what I am saying very carefully and pass these words on to those who could not be present here today, for those absent might better understand and keep the words well.

❧

"O people,
just as this day, this month, and this city are sacred, your life, property, and chastity are sacred and inviolable to each other. They are secure from any offensive.

❧

"Remember!
Tomorrow you will meet your Lord and answer for your deeds. So beware: do not stray from the path of righteousness after I am gone by slaying each other.

"Return the goods entrusted to you to their rightful owners. God has forbidden you to be involved in usury; therefore all interest obligations shall henceforth be waived. Your capital is yours to keep. You will neither inflict nor suffer any inequity. God has judged that there shall be no interest and the first interest that I waive is that due to Abbas ibn Abdulmuttalib.[1]

৯৯৯

"Every right arising out of homicide in pre-Islamic days is henceforth nullified and the first such right that I nullify is that arising from the murder of Rabiah.[2]

৯৯৯

"Truly, the hereditary distinctions that were pretensions to respect in the Age of Ignorance have been laid aside forever, except for the custodianship of the Ka'ba (by Bani 'Abd al-Dar) and the giving of drink to pilgrims (by al-'Abbas).

৯৯৯

"A deliberate murder is subject to retaliation in kind.[3] An accidental death from a deliberate injury means a death resulting from (an instrument that is not usually used or intended as a deadly weapon, such as) a stick or a rock; the indemnity for this is one hundred camels.[4] Whoever asks for more is a person from the Age of Ignorance.

৯৯৯

"Beware of Satan...
Satan has lost all his influence and authority in this land. But he is content to be obeyed in matters which you deem of little significance. Beware of Satan for the safety of your religion.

৯৯৯

"O people!
Watch over the rights of women, and fear God in this respect. Remember that you have taken them as your wives only under

---

[1] The Prophet's uncle.
[2] The Prophet's nephew.
[3] Any punishment is under the authority of a central government. Individuals cannot retaliate.
[4] Camel was one of the most significant components of 7th-century Arab civilization, which was the best mode of transportation under desert conditions in that age.

God's trust and with His permission. And it is your right that they protect the honor of the family and that they do not let anyone you dislike into your house without your permission. Women also have rights over you that you must provide for them and clothe them as befits the society.

‎

"I leave behind me such a trust that if you hold tight onto it you will never go astray. It is the Qur'an, the book of God.

‎

"O people!

Postponing the inviolability of a sacred month is a surfeit of unbelief; in this way are those who disbelieve led astray. They make it lawful one year and unlawful in another; this is in order to match the number (of months) God has made inviolable.[5] Time has verily come full turn, to how it was when the day God created the heavens and the Earth. With God the months are twelve in number. Four of them are holy, three of these are successive and one occurs singly between the months of Jumada and Shaban.

‎

"O believers!

Listen to my words carefully and keep them. Believers are but brothers and sisters. Nothing which belongs to a believer shall be legitimate to a fellow believer unless it is given freely and willingly. O my Companions! Do not do injustice to your selves, for your selves have rights over you too.

‎

---

[5]   In order to postpone the ban on killing that occurs in three months of the Muslim calendar, some people would interpret dates differently, when it suited them. This would insure that they would not be in violation of the rules during a sacred month, and they could carry on with a battle, even if the sacred month had arrived; consequently the regular course of calendar was often changed.

"Your Lord is one, and your father is one: all of you are of Adam, and Adam was of soil. An Arab has no superiority over a non-Arab—except by piety and good action.[6]

৯~৯

"O people,

God has apportioned to every deserving heir his share of the estate, and no deserving heir may accept a special bequest, and no special bequest (to anyone else) may exceed a third of the estate.

৯~৯

"A child's lineage is that of the (husband who owns the) bed, and adulterers shall be deprived of the child. Whoever claims to be the son of someone besides his father or a bondsman who claims to belong to other than his masters shall bear the curse of God and the angels and all believers; neither their proclamation nor their repentance shall be accepted.

৯~৯

"Be my witness, O God, that I have conveyed Your message to Your people."

---

[6] Although the Prophet gives Arabs as an example, he is addressing to the fact that no race is superior to any other race.

If greatness of purpose, smallness of means, and astounding results
are the three criteria of human genius, who could dare to compare
any great man in modern history with Muhammad?

Lamartine

PRAISE FOR THE PROPHET

Jane Louise Kandur

L ike Alphonse de Lamartine, many in the West have come to respect and appreciate the Prophet Muhammad, peace and blessings be upon him. Such appreciaton is based upon research, careful analysis, comparative work, and sound conclusions. By contrast, the 2005 "cartoon crisis" that began in Denmark and that eventually erupted around the world, was the product of prejudice, ignorance, and distortion, which was due in part to the artists of these cartoons accepting the distorted view of Islam as it is presented by some extremists. In reality, extremists of this sort are not unique to Islam.[7] Freedom of speech is an essential component of being human, however, abusing this freedom for sarcasm and humiliating others, especially in a time filled with crises, is hurtful, shamel, and disrespectful, thus unacceptable. The offenders who had drawn the cartoons would probably not have drawn the Blessed Prophet with a bomb in his turban if they had heard what Mahatma Gandhi had to say about him:

> I wanted to know the best of one who holds today undisputed
> sway over the hearts of millions of mankind . . . I became more
> than convinced that it was not the sword that won a place for
> Islam in those days in the scheme of life. It was the rigid sim-

---

[7] On September 30, 2005, *Jyllands-Posten*, a Danish newspaper published cartoons in which the Prophet was depicted in an offensive caricature. Offended Muslims all over the world held marches and boycotts to protest this publication which was later published by other European newspapers.

plicity, the utter self-effacement of the Prophet, the scrupulous regard for his pledges, his intense devotion to his friends and followers, his intrepidity, his fearlessness, his absolute trust in God and in his own mission. These and not the sword carried everything before them and surmounted every obstacle. When I closed the 2nd volume (of the Prophet's biography), I was sorry there was not more for me to read of the great life.

Lamartine complemented the above epigram as follows:

The most famous of men are those who created arms, laws, and empires. They founded, if anything at all, no more than material powers which often crumbled away before their eyes. This man moved not only armies, legislations, empires, peoples, and dynasties, but millions of men in one-third of the then inhabited world; and more than that, he moved the altars, the gods, the religions, the ideas, the beliefs and souls...his forbearance in victory, his ambition, which was entirely devoted to one idea and in no manner striving for an empire; his endless prayers, his mystic conversations with God, his death and his triumph after death; all these attest not to an imposture but to a firm conviction which gave him the power to restore a dogma. This dogma was two-fold, the unity of God and the immateriality of God; the former telling what God is, the latter telling what God is not; the one overthrowing false gods with the sword, the other starting an idea with the words. Philosopher, orator, apostle, legislator, warrior, conqueror of ideas, restorer of rational dogmas, of a cult without images, the founder of twenty terrestrial empires and of one spiritual empire; that is MUHAMMAD. As regards all the standards by which Human Greatness may be measured, we may well ask, IS THERE ANY MAN GREATER THAN HE? (*Historie de la Turquie*, Paris, 1854, Vol. II, pp. 276-277).

In 1974, Dr. Jules Masserman, an American psychoanalyst, carried out a study entitled "Who Were Histories Great Leaders?" As reported in *Time* magazine, when focusing on great spiritual leaders, Dr. Masserman asked three analytical questions: 1) Did he provide his community with well-being? 2) Was he able to construct a social organization where his followers could feel safe? 3) Did he manage to draw up a comprehensive scheme of faith. Masserman concluded that "perhaps the greatest leader of all times was Muhammad, who combined all the three functions. To a lesser degree Moses did the same."

In 1978, in his *The 100: Ranking of the Most Influential Persons in History*, Michael H. Hart notes:

> My choice of Muhammad to lead the list of the world's most influential persons may surprise some readers and may be questioned by others, but he was the only man in history who was supremely successful on both the religious and secular level.

According to Thomas Carlyle, a Scottish historian and essayist, the Prophet Muhammad is exceptional, in that, he single-handedly weld warring tribes and wandering Bedouins into a most powerful and civilized nation in less than two decades. In his *The Hero as a Prophet* Carlyle described the Prophet as a "silent and magnificent soul."

In their *History of the Saracen Empires* (London, 1870) Edward Gibbon and Simon Ockley speak on the profession of Islam:

> "I believe in one God, and Mahomet, an apostle of God" is the simple and invariable profession of Islam. The intellectual image of the Deity has never been degraded by any visible idol; the honor of the Prophet have never transgresses the measure of human virtues; and his living precepts have restrained the gratitude of his disciples within the bounds of reason and religion.

Sir George Bernard Shaw said: "I have studied this wonderful man and I think that he was far from being an antichrist. I feel compelled to call him the savior of mankind . . . If a man like Muhammad were to assume the dictatorship of the modern world, he would succeed in solving its problems that would bring it the much needed peace and happiness."

Johann Wolfgang von Goethe also paid tribute to the Prophet Muhammad. Fascination of Islam and its founder took hold of Goethe at a young age and occupied him to the extent that he could not shake it off for the remainder of his life. The 70 year old Goethe confessed openly that he was thinking to "reverentially celebrate that holy night the Qur'an was sent down to the Prophet from above." With his *West-Eastern Divan* he set up a literary monument to Islam. One of his self written announcements for this book even comprises the astonishing sentence that the author of the book wouldn't argue if he "were suspected of being a Muslim himself" (quoted from Die Welt, February 11, 2006).

The following praise and final analysis by W. Montgomery Watt in his *Mohammad at Mecca* (Oxford, 1953) explains why we have such offenses as we have today:

> His readiness to undergo persecutions for his beliefs, the high moral character of the men who believed in him and looked up to him as leader, and the greatness of his ultimate achievement— all argue his fundamental integrity. To suppose Muhammad an impostor raises more problems than it solves. Moreover, none of the great figures of history is so poorly appreciated in the West as Muhammad.

SAMPLES OF POETRY DEDICATED TO THE PROPHET

The Rose of Medina

M. Fethullah Gülen

Whenever I commemorate You, all else fades from my mind,
Your phantasm treads on the hills of my mind;
Although a mirage, it assuages my affliction,
Whenever I commemorate You, all else fades from my mind.

I wish your love pervade each second of my life,
And I could soar like spirits and circumambulate your aurora,
And find some way to ooze into your heart,
I wish your love pervade each second of my life.

I avow it is too late to attain your blissful presence,
My heart will ceaselessly be lamenting still,
Forever anticipating you with the freshest hopes,
I avow it is too late to attain your blissful presence,

As my heart flutters like a dove, hankering for you,
I beg you to grant me a plume of yours!
So that I could flap after you forever,
As my heart flutters like a dove, hankering for you.

O Rose that turns scorching desert into Eden!
Come and lapse flow into my soul with your enchanting colors!
It is high time your smiles shone on the apples of my eyes.
O Rose that turns scorching desert into Eden!

જ ન્ઝ

Let me be your slave, like Majnun, in the quest for you,
Sprinkle embers on my soul, let me burn like a furnace.
And be relieved of this rancorous dream elapsing without you,
Let me be your slave, like Majnun, in the quest for you.

જ ન્ઝ

I count the days I have been severed from you,
That coils about my soul like gloomy dolor.
Let me see your face before the twilight unfolds,
I count the days I have been severed from you.

જ ન્ઝ

Let me see my dusk turn into dawn at my last gasp,
And my heart be filled with the newest colors of your horizon,
Lutes would be resounding then, and flutes would be heard,
Let me see my dusk turn into dawn at my last gasp.

Translated from Turkish by Metin Boşnak

Black Locks

Mehmet Erdoğan

You shot me in the heart, set me on fire,
The only rose of my fate, sweet musk-scented hair

My enshrouding sphere, You bestow abundantly,
Wings of the angel lay down for you on the way to the Lote-tree.[1]

The Station of Two-Bows' Length, the highest peak of all,
You are the breath of the original nature,[2] the cosmos' lofty call.

You are the rain of mercy and compassion from the most Supreme,
You are the Master of existence, prior even to Adam.

O the Ocean of Light! Would your grace cascade from a fountain?
The myriads of hearts would each become for you a crystal pool.

Black Locks you must be called, O the Beloved,
I wonder if my cry can reach you, dull, enfeebled.

My troubles are far too many, and I myself possess no cures at all,
I spent summers in vain, and am left in poverty in the fall.

---

[1] *sidrat al-muntaha*: (the Lote-tree of the Boundary) a station which the Prophet was raised during his Ascension.

[2] *fitrat*: the original state in which humans are created by God

"Perhaps a hand will be extended," I thought, "if I knock on your door,"
"Perhaps my Master could find a cure for this sinner."

I am afraid to hear you say, "Who is he?"
Then, all abodes would become a dungeon for me.

You are a cure for troubles, let this heart burn,
O the Beloved of the Merciful; to ashes let it burn.

Moons split at your command,[3]
Nothing but a full moon is seen in your face.

Purest water pours down from your fingers quenching armies,[4]
The hardest hearts soften in rapture with your breath.

Your blessed saliva is a heavenly river and a salve for the wounded,
Every moment in your company is time spent in heaven.

Black Locks I say, for the color of the Hira cave
Is united in harmony with that of the Miraj night.

Hajar al-Asad[5] is imbued in black,
Inspired by the black of your hair, O the Beloved with rosebud lips.

---

3 One of the well known miracles of the Prophet was "splitting the moon." Once, the most staunched idolaters of Mecca came and asked him to show them a miracle to prove his mission. The Prophet prayed and the moon split. One half of the moon appeared above a mountain while the other half appeared above another mountain. This miracle is confirmed by the following verse: *The Hour has approached and the moon split* (Qamar 54:1).

4 This verse refers to one of the Prophet's miracles. The Prophet dipped his fingers into a pot of water and immediately after he took them out, from each water flowed like a fountain.

5 Hajar al-Asad is the black stone that is found in one of the corners of the Ka'ba in Mecca. Pilgrims start circumambulation from the corner on which this stone is placed.

Black Locks I say, for the pitch black of the Ka'ba,
Draining the color of your eyes, as if from Kawthar.

෨ ෩

O *Black Locks*, come before laments are no longer of use,
O *Black Locks*, come before my life comes to a close.

෨ ෩

O *Black Locks*, come before my love fades in my heart,
O *Black Locks*, come before the Angel descends to take this life away.
With sparkling light, bestow upon me the horizons of future,
May all the horror on the road change into glory.

෨ ෩

Burying my face into your prints in the dust,
Burning in flames, crying your name "O Muhammad!"

෨ ෩

I wish to reach the land beyond, thirsty and tired,
On my lips, may cries of "water" and "Lord" become entwined.

෨ ෩

Perhaps my burning could be the lowest of mercy,
A kiss from an angel whispering "He" while touching.

෨ ෩

O *Black Locks*, all my days roam in this way,
Each ordeal passes engulfed in longing for you.

෨ ෩

Stop this pain, put an end to this longing,
Uproot and hurl away this torment of separation from my heart.

෨ ෩

Hurl it away to the unknown or to extermination,
Burn this heart forever with your light of reunion.

My Soul Is In Love with You

Ali Ulvi Kurucu

My soul is in love with you and in admiration, O Master!

Not only I, but the whole world is at your disposal O Master!

Planets and stars, the works of the Lord's pen; I adore watching them,

But the Lord, the Creator of all good, is in love with your face, O Master!

At the Doomsday, even the Prophets seek help from you,

The Merciful calls you "the mercy for all worlds," O Master!

Every night, the moans of the lovers rise up to the Divine Throne,

The Qur'an praises your good character, O Master.

My heart burns like a censer for your love.

I would suffer longing even in Paradise if without you.

Rise into my soul, O the light that consoles my heart,

Your light is the healing for the disease in my heart.

Ulvi is burning in the heart, your weeping lover.

His cry is nothing but a blazing fire, O Master.

We are your guarding servants, O Master, do not dismiss us,

Your grace to the rebels is a divine command, O Master.

Pearls of Wisdom

- Humanity came to know true civilization by means of the Prophet Muhammad, upon him be peace and blessings, and favored it. All efforts exerted after him for the sake of true civilization have been no more than practicing or trying to practice the principles he brought and adjusting them to new conditions. For this reason, he deserves to be called the founder of true civilization.

- The Prophet Muhammad, upon him be peace and blessings, rejected indolence and the lazy and esteemed labor as a mode of worship and applauded the hard-working. He directed his followers to horizons beyond the age in which they lived and taught them how they cold be the element of balance in of balance in the world.

- The Prophet Muhammad, upon him be peace and blessings, is unequalled in that he appeared as a sword of valor and eloquence against unbelief and savagery. He proclaimed the truth with the clearest voice and showed mankind the ways to true existence.

- If there is ever a person whom ignorance, unbelief and brutality hate the most, it is Muhammad, upon him be peace and blessings. Those who search for truth and thirst for true knowledge eventually will seek him out and embrace his path.

- The Prophet Muhammad, upon him be peace and blessings, proclaimed true freedom to humanity, and ingrained in human consciousness that all human beings are equal before the law. He established that superiority lies in virtue, piety, and morality. He regarded proclaiming the truth against all oppressors and oppressive thought as a kind of worship.

- The Prophet Muhammad, upon him be peace and blessings, called upon us to protect religion, life, reason, property and the integrity of family and lineage, and to strive for this purpose. In a remarkably balanced way, he proclaimed that no other duty could equal this struggle.

- The Prophet Muhammad, upon him be peace and blessings, unveiled the transitory nature of this world and death, and showed the grave to be a waiting room opening onto the realm of eternal happiness. He led every heart seeking happiness, regardless of place or time, to the fountain of Khidr, and enabled them to drink the elixir of immortality.

THE LIFE OF THE PROPHET IN CHRONOLOGICAL ORDER

Mecca Period

571	- The birth of the Prophet (April 20, Monday). Another possible date is June 17, 569.
	- He was given to Halima to be suckled and weaned.
574	- Halima brought him back to Mecca to his mother, Amina.
575	- Amina died, Abdulmuttalib, his grandfather, assumed custody.
577	- Abdulmuttalib died. His uncle Abu Talib became his guardian.
578	- First trip to Syria with Abu Talib.
589 (?)	- Took oath for Hilf al-Fudl (Pact of Excellence).
594	- He led Khadija's trade caravan to Busra.
	- Marriage with Khadija.
605	- Arbitration between different clans in the crisis of restoring the Black Stone to the Ka'ba.
610	- The first revelation in the cave of Hira in the month of Ramadan (the first five verses of chapter Alaq).
613	- First public summon to Islam. He invited his nearest of kin to the faith.
614	- Pagans of Mecca started torturing weak Muslims.
615	- First emigration in Islam. Some Companions set off to Abyssinia.
616	- Second emigration to Abyssinia.
	- Hamza and Umar embraced Islam
	- Pagans started a social and economic boycott to the clan of the Prophet
619	- Boycott ended.
620	- The year of sadness. Khadija and Abu Talib died.
	- Visited Ta'if to teach Islam.

          - A group of pilgrims from Medina (then Yathrib) met the Prophet and embraced Islam.

621   - The miracle of the Ascension (Miraj) and the prescribed daily prayers commanded.

          - First Aqaba Pledge with a group from Medina and the assignation of Mus'ab ibn Umayr by the Prophet to teach Islam there.

622   - Second Aqaba Pledge.

Medina Period

622   - Muslims started emigration to Medina.

          - Meccan leaders plotted to murder the Prophet.

          - The Prophet emigrated to Medina with Abu Bakr.

          - The building of Masjid al-Nabawi (the Prophet's mosque) started.

          - Adhan, call to prayer, introduced.

623   - Brotherhood established between the Emigrants and Helpers (*muahat*).

          - The Medina Contract drawn and the borders of the city determined.

          - A marketplace established in the city.

624   - Direction of prayer changed from Masjid al-Aqsa in Jerusalem to Ka'ba in Mecca.

          - Obligatory fasting in Ramadan started.

          - The Battle of Badr.

          - Marriage with Aisha.

          - Ali married Fatima, the Prophet's daughter.

          - Festivities of Ramadan and sacrifice observed for the first time.

          - Prescribed alms commanded.

625   - The Battle of Uhud.

          - Alcohol forbidden.

627   - Census in Medina.

          - The Battle of the Trench.

628   - Hudaybiya Peace Treaty and the revelation of the chapter Fath (conquest).

- Letters sent to emperors of the Byzantium and Sasanid Empires, as well as to the rulers of other neighboring countries.
- Ashama, the Negus (king) of Abyssinia, embraced Islam.
- Expedition to Haybar.
- Zainab bint Harith attempted to poison the Prophet.

629
- Khalid b. Walid, Amr b. As, and Uthman b. Talha embraced Islam.
- The Battle of Mu'tah.
- Hudaybiya Peace Treaty violated by Meccan pagans.

630
- The conquest of Mecca.
- The Battle of Hunayn.
- Funeral for Ashama observed by the Prophet in absentia.
- The Battle of Tabuk.
- A second letter of invitation to Islam sent to Heraclius, the emperor of Byzantium.
- Ka'b b. Zuhayr (the poet of Ode the Mantle) embraced Islam. The Prophet gave his mantle as a gift to him.

631
- Death of Abdullah bin Ubayy, a prominent hypocrite.
- The hajj, major pilgrimage, commanded.
- A committee of Christians from Najran visited the Prophet.
- The Prophet took a twenty-day spiritual retreat in Ramadan and recited the Qur'an twice with Gabriel.
- Musaylima, the liar, asserted a self-claimed prophethood.

632
- The farewell pilgrimage and sermon.
- The Prophet died, Monday, June 8 (Rabi al-awwal 13).

INDEX